What others are saying about We Were Reborn for

My friend Britt has written a straightforward, challenging, and transformative book on living a reborn life on this earth following a Jesus model. His work in *We were Reborn for This* is important for all Christians to read and absorb. Thank you Britt for this profound work.

Bishop Garland Hunt, Senior Pastor of the Father's House, Peachtree Corners, GA

Who better than Lazarus to reveal what a radically reborn life looks like? Get ready to discover the deeper story Jesus created you for in a way that will reawaken your hopes, heart, and imagination!

Allen Arnold, Author of *The Story of With* and *The Eden Option*

This isn't a book. This is a conversation with a friend—a fellow Christian—that delves into the subjects of finding intimacy with Christ and our purpose once we come to Him and He to us. This is a treasure chest you'll open more than once.

Eva Marie Everson, CEO, Word Weavers International, Author: *The Third Path*

This book reminds believers that the Gospel is far more than an invitation to spend eternity in heaven. It's an invitation to get involved in God's epic story of redeeming mankind to live with Him now. We have been re-born for this purpose! A must-read for anyone who asks, "What is God's will for my life?"

Grace Fox, co-director of International Messengers Canada, podcaster, author of *Fresh Hope for Today: Devotions for Joy on the Journey*

What can i say, this book is gold! Britt's understanding and explanation of biblical principles in a way anyone can understand rejuvenates the passion in believers and reaches unbelievers where they are. I loved everything about this book, especially the stories!

Michael J. Lewis - Child of God, Husband, Father, and Author of *True Worth: Identity in Christ*

Not only does Britt live out his faith unashamedly, he has a compassion for others and a teacher's heart that makes listening to him discuss Scripture a pleasure.

Bethany Jett, author of Platinum Faith and Navigating Minefields

We Were Reborn for This should be required reading for all Christians. So often we get stuck on the wrong side of the cross, living in false humility that we are totally unworthy. We were. But to remain in that mindset after Christ's great sacrifice to forgive us and make us friends and co-heirs with Him actually steals and demeans what His work accomplished, robbing Him of His glory.

Bill Myers, author of *Rendezvous with God*, a novel, Volumes 1-4

Britt Mooney is an incredible author, Pastor, and friend. The Kingdom thanks you for the contribution of this book.

Sebastian Holley PhD lead of Unity Global Network.

Britt Mooney is a man who exemplifies what it means to live heaven on earth through his unwavering commitment to love and serve God and people. We Were Reborn For This is an important reminder to the Church that we exist to serve this world and bring heaven to earth through a relentless demonstration of God's love and power.

Duke Lamastra, Executive Pastor, Legacy Church International Author, *Simple Power*

BRITT MOONEY

THE JESUS MODEL FOR LIVING HEAVEN ON EARTH

We Were REBORN for This

The Jesus Model for Living Heaven on Earth

Britt Mooney

Bold Vision Books
PO Box 2011
Friendswood, TX 77549

Copyright © Britt Mooney 2023

ISBN
Library of Congress Control Number

All rights reserved.
Published by Bold Vision Books, PO Box 2011, Friendswood, Texas 77549
www.boldvisionbooks.com

Published in association with literary agent Cyle Young Literary Elite.

Cover Design by Amber Weigand-Buckley
Edited by Cherry D. McGregor
Interior design by *k*ae Creative Solutions

Published in the United States of America.

All rights reserved. No part of this publication may be reproduced, stored in a retrieval system, or transmitted in any form or by any means—electronic, mechanical, photocopy, recording, or any other—except for brief quotations in printed reviews, without the prior permission of the publisher.

Unless otherwise noted, all Scripture quotations are taken from the Holy Bible, New Living Translation, (NLT) copyright ©1996, 2004, 2007 by Tyndale House Foundation. Used by permission of Tyndale House Publishers, Inc., Carol Stream, Illinois 60188. All rights reserved.

Dedication

To all the Kingdom Misfits born of Heaven.

You are gifts from God, and we need you.

Table of Contents

Foreword

Introduction

1. Never Heard that Before
2. The Jesus Model
3. Rule #1: Don't Freak Out

ONE – CROW: Roll Away the Stone

4. Nothing but Love
5. Redemptive Justice
6. Unity
7. Dignity, Relief, Empowerment
8. Supernatural Expression
9. Walk in Righteousness
10. The Story of the Gospel

TWO – FLY: Life from the Dead

11. The Work of God
12. Death to Life
13. New Creation
14. Made Free
15. Rest & Purpose
16. Eternal Inheritance
17. New People

THREE – FIGHT: Unwrapping the Gift

18. Discipline of Relationship
19. Power of Community

20. Remove the Old
21. Reveal the New
22. Purpose of the Disciplines
23. The Mission
24. The War

Now I *Knower* It

Acknowledgments

Meet Britt Mooney

Foreword

Isaiah prophesied of the very times in which we live saying, "Arise, shine; for your light is come, and the glory of the Lord is risen upon thee. For behold, the darkness shall cover the earth, and thick darkness the people: but the Lord shall arise upon you, and His glory shall be seen upon you".

Darkness represents the deception and false narratives of Lucifer's attempts to confuse every person. Light is God's reality arising on those to whom He makes it known, It fills the humble who seek the source of truth: the Father, to whom Jesus bowed saying, "Thine is the Kingdom, and the power, and the glory, forever".

Britt Mooney, in his book *We Were Reborn For This*, writes with stirring insight to born-again believers. He declares the set apart church are carriers of this Divine intent to help rescue those in thick darkness, recognizing the importance of one soul or ten thousand.

Such illumination shining through humble yet courageous vessels releases those bound by Lucifer's lie of: this world is all there is. Individuals are able to conquer this falsehood by the greater power in being born again, able now to see and engage what is presently coming from the Kingdom realm of heaven.

This book is timely for it enlightens from Scripture God's prophetic purpose. It shows that the Father's desire to reach all who are lost without eternal perspective is already preset in the church His Son is building.

By Providential wisdom, those learning to align with Christ's activity inside their spirit have His Divine capacity to arise at this time in history. We were reborn for this! In the years I have been privileged to know Britt Mooney, his integrity and consistency have always challenged me toward the Father's greater plan, opening further my thoughts to the broader counsel of God's will. Britt has also helped many others to set their pursuit on the

Kingdom, thereby receiving the overcoming ability inherent in it. *We Were Reborn For This* is fully supplied with these declarations of Kingdom reality. It is not for the faint at heart, or maybe it is, for it will strengthen the courage of each reader who, after counting the cost, still desires to embrace the essential task at hand. The American Church is entering one of its most challenging periods in her history. Our battle is most real, at times formidable, because the eternal stakes are very high. These are days of victorious clarity concerning "What is Truth?".

Britt has put in writing for us a hopeful and joyous understanding that the Kingdom of heaven and knowing the Father is the focal point of reality. He pens many specifics of this, as you will read, exhorting the awakening Church onward to their triumphant purpose and calling.

~Chris Strong, Pastor

Introduction

*P*eter, don't you know who you are?"

The house is dark and quiet, two children sleeping in beds, left in the care of a nanny while their parents are out at a fancy dinner. Everything seems safe.

This is the moment when evil and chaos enter the home. A villain travels from another realm and breaks into the house, causing terror. The nanny cowers, screaming, and the bad guy kidnaps the kids, Maggie and Jack.

The parents, Peter and Moira, return to the home along with Grandma Wendy, and they find their home in crisis, glass shattered. The lights don't work, the door wide open, and the children gone. In shock, they realize that the kidnapper has left a note requesting Peter's presence, a challenge to come and save the children.

It is signed by someone named Hook.

Right away, an old man says something crazy. "Have to fly. Have to fight. Have to crow. Have to save Maggie. Have to save Jack."

Peter and Moira do what anyone would do. Call the police. The authorities are their only hope, right? The police can only take the information and leave.

Later, Grandma Wendy urgently has a conversation with Peter, the dad. "The stories are true. I swear to you," she says. "The fight isn't over with James Hook ... only you can save your children."

Peter is afraid and confused. What is this old woman talking about?

With frustration and longing in her voice, Granny Wendy says, "Peter, don't you know who you are?"

Peter is the fairy-tale hero, Peter Pan, and she is Wendy from those narratives. He has forgotten his identity.

But he must remember. To save and love his kids, he needs to embrace who he truly is. He's the only one who can.

That was a scene in a movie, though *Hook* is a fictional story.

What we're dealing with is real.

The Chaos

Chaos surrounds us on all sides. On a meta level, the division in our world has only increased. The conflicts have only deepened, becoming more hateful and toxic despite desperate calls for unity and healing. Whether cultural clashes, racial violence and unrest, political posturing and corrupt agendas, the plight of the poor, the abuse of children, or an international pandemic, we hurtle down a wide path to destruction.

What can we do? It's too big. Too much.

The hopelessness doesn't diminish when we consider our individual lives. I can scroll past the crisis or click-bait headlines and emotionally distance myself from wars and politicians. But when my child needs counseling for suicidal thoughts, I can't ignore that. Chaos doesn't stay out there in the world where we view it through a computer screen. The tragedy and crisis steal into my home, as well.

Chaos gets personal. Spouses cheat and leave, loved ones take their own lives, people we care about get addicted to drugs, a family member is paralyzed in an accident, or a close friend is diagnosed with a chronic illness.

We want to help. We do. However, we also know the evil and selfishness of our hearts and thoughts, our inability to make the slightest change in our own behavior, much less change the story of a family member, far less to end homelessness in the world.

We feel powerless.

On one level, we try to deal with it like anyone would, appealing to the powers of this world to help. But we quickly realize our leaders and systems can only place band aids, or perhaps they are part of the problem. We accept this as the way it is. The best we can do is hope for pain or crisis management.

However, if this is the best, why do we hope for a perfect world where children aren't raped or killed, where families have homes, and where the poor aren't oppressed? It isn't a world we've ever seen with our eyes, yet we long for it. While entities like government, culture, religion, entertainment, and education have their place, they aren't the solution. If they could fix the brokenness of this world, they would have by now.

We long for a loving and healing world that seems impossible. God, however, specializes in doing the impossible.

Invasion of Hope

God loved the world so very much that he provided a solution to the hopelessness, the darkness, the division, and the self-destruction within our hearts and the world. He sent his only begotten Son, the Lord Jesus Christ.

The method of solution was *incarnation*. God became a human to be with us so we could be with him. With this incarnation of a person, the Kingdom of God invaded our world of chaos. Invasions through history are by force, deception, violence. Not this one. This invasion conquers by invitation, truth, and love. God with us.

Jesus raised up an army of love and truth to continue the invasion, but we must be clear on the method. The very nature of God within humanity continued with the apostles and the church. Incarnation didn't stop with Jesus; it spread from Jerusalem across borders and cultures and languages, a people full of God performing wonders and miracles. A growing army of love that turned the world upside down.

Do we really believe the stories in the Bible happened? Are these scriptures only myths or fairy tales in a book for nice moral lessons or intellectual argument in theological debate? Maybe a few special people with a title can live a story of miracle, but not the rest of us, right? We're just trying to survive, after all. We don't have time for a revolution. Especially one so difficult to believe. We have other responsibilities.

I understand why it's difficult to believe. We are intimately aware of our lack, our own corruption. We are broken vessels more likely to mess it up or make it worse if we even try to be like heroes in an ancient tome. Sometimes we can't pay our bills, much less bring hope to a dying world. Giving hope is for someone else.

Except that's a lie. It is for us, if we will only believe. The stories in the Bible are real, and the reborn are the only people who can bring light to darkness, peace to the chaos, and life to death. Not to manage chaos but destroy it, undo it. As Rich Mullins said, "What I think is scary about God is he didn't come up with any plan B. That he left the Church here, and the Church is the only group of people, and the Church is the only institution in the world that can bring about a change."

God in us to the world is the revolution. Jesus in plumbers and doctors and teachers and the dude working at the drive thru. Worldly position doesn't matter. The power of God in us matters.

Identity is powerful. When we know who and whose we are, everything flows from that—purpose, meaning, hope, joy, peace, contentment, and more.

I feel much like Wendy from *Hook*.

The message of God to his people, and subsequently this book, is this:

"Do we know who we are?"

The world still desperately needs to be turned upside down, a revolution of hope.

Incarnation, God in humanity, is the Father's solution. The only one. "You must be born again," Jesus said (John 3:3-7). Why? For the Kingdom, he told Nicodemus late at night. To see and enter the world we long for, we must be *re*born.

The world doesn't need another mega-church pastor, political revolutionary, cultural icon, genius entertainer, or best-selling author. We need a new people. We weren't reconciled with the Father and born of God simply to escape hell. That is a necessary part of the process, but we have a greater purpose, to live heaven on earth and invite others into the same.

There have been moments where I've been involved in an activity and felt such satisfaction and meaning I thought, "I was born to do this." That is a taste of what God wants for us. To bring the revolution of hope, light, and love to the world and experience eternal contentment and joy through all believers living on earth like heaven is real.

We were *re*born for this.

Chapter 1
Never Heard that Before

I sat with Bill at the kitchen table during a party where several different types of games were played throughout the house. Bill and I were busy with a board game between us.

Bill asked a spiritual question, and the conversation turned. His inquiry caught the attention of many in the kitchen, especially a young man eager to defend Christian ideals. I said little, taking my cues from God for what to say.

After the eager young man finished, Bill said, "Yeah, I've heard all that before. I went to every kind of church as a kid. I've heard it all."

The young man had to excuse himself as his toddler began to scream and get in trouble.

In a moment of vulnerability, Bill turned to me. "Here's what I see. The world is hanging by a thread and could all fall apart at any moment. I've seen some really dark things in my life. I should be dead. My question is, why am I still alive? Why am I here?"

I grinned. "I could answer, but it will take some time."

He agreed to listen.

For the next twenty minutes, I spoke amidst the background noise of zapping and gunfire from the video games in the next room. This is a summary.

The world is in chaos, without form and void, when God comes on the scene in Genesis. He speaks light into darkness, form into formlessness. That's who God is and what he does.

When humanity messed up and brought death and corruption into the world, God's solution was again to enter the spiritual darkness through his Son, Jesus. Life himself entered the dying, wicked world to bring life, hope, and peace.

"You are still here for a reason, Bill. You have talents and skills. If you give your life to Jesus, God will redeem those talents, give you meaning and purpose, entering the lives of other people who have known dark things. Then you can bring light into their darkness, peace into their chaos. That is why you're still alive."

He stared at me for a long time. "I've never heard that before."

He's not the only one who hasn't heard that before. It wasn't the first time I'd shared the message or one similar with different narratives or approaches. Even those who have been Christians for decades give me a blank gaze in return. They've heard great teaching and encouragement, but when faced with the power and purpose of being born again, it's a foreign concept.

This message, though, pulls on our hearts because it addresses our deepest longings.

What We Long for Most

We need physical resources like food and clothing to survive in this world, but we believe a lie to think material things, and more of them, will satisfy the core longings of our heart.

I once desired to be a rock star and religiously watched the cable TV show *Behind the Music*. Every episode was a documentary on a different pop or rock artist. A pattern emerged. The musician was poor and struggling and they sacrificed everything to get what they desired—success wrapped in fame and wealth.

In every case but one, the artists would achieve their goals and invariably find their lives empty and meaningless. Wealth and fame only became another form of slavery, and they would turn to drugs and alcohol or another vice to bring emotional relief or artificially manufacture the satisfaction they sought, which, of course, didn't work.

These talented individuals would spiral in self-destructive behavior until they realized those external goals were never the path to find what they longed for most. Tragically, some would die to overdoses or accidents, but for those that survived and realized what was important, they discovered love with family, generosity, reconciliation, faith in God, or helping others.

The one exception I saw was Huey Lewis. He had experienced the heartbreak in the industry before and knew any fame or success was temporary, and he treated it as such.

These artists rediscovered the two things humanity longs for more than anything else. Intimacy and purpose.

It should make complete sense that those made in God's image need intimacy and purpose. God is, within himself, an intimate family relationship. It is the mystery of the Trinity, three distinct persons who are also one in a beautiful harmony beyond our imagination.

> **This is what we long for and what God provides in the Gospel. Intimacy and purpose..**

He is also a God of purpose, always and continually active with intent unto good. We see his goodness from his introduction in Genesis throughout every situation in Scripture. His intimacy and purpose culminated in sending Jesus as the ultimate solution to save that which was lost.

God with us through incarnation. And with purpose—to undo the works of the Devil.

Jesus expressed this Good News the following way. "Repent of your sins and turn to God, for the Kingdom of Heaven is near." (Matthew 4:17) This is what Jesus preached, what the Scripture calls the Gospel of the Kingdom. Turn our lives to God, be reborn, walk in his presence, and live heaven on earth. This is what we long for and what God provides in the Gospel. Intimacy and purpose.

God's purpose, what he is doing, simply stated, is this: *The Father is reconciling all creation to himself through his Son, the Lord Jesus Christ.*

(1 Corinthians 15:20-26) The goal of his purpose is intimacy, and he's making all things new along the way (Revelation 21:5).

A quick note. We can't separate intimacy and purpose, like we can't separate the heart from the lungs and still live. They are inescapably linked in God's nature. Purpose without intimacy brings legalism (what we do), and intimacy without purpose brings lasciviousness (what feels good). Either without the other isn't just an incomplete picture of God, it isn't a picture of God at all. We can be drawn to one extreme because of our personality or culture, but to separate intimacy and purpose leads to bad doctrine and lies about God.

We shouldn't give pop and rock artists a hard time, though. The same deception tempts the church.

A Different Measure and Goal

Beginning in 2020, the world went through great upheaval. COVID-19 spread unseen across borders and shut down the societies and economies of entire nations, throwing us into crisis.

Churches closed their doors, whether voluntarily or by force, and spiritual leaders scrambled for how to best serve their congregation and community. Worship went streaming, many for the first time. Others set up drive-in services.

During the crisis and initial shutdown, I was invited to meet online with pastors to discuss how to work together and bring relief to those in need, an amazing and encouraging expression of the local Body of Christ. The administrative pastor of one of the largest churches in Georgia shared how they had to adjust to changes during the shutdowns. His church was massive, the standard of achievement for many in the American church.

The mega-church pastor explained, "None of our measures of success work anymore. They are all out the window."

I know several in leadership of this church and other congregations like it. They absolutely love Jesus and have a heart to see people changed and transformed. His frustration was real.

What measures was he referring to? Specifically, attendance to programs or services and money raised.

The pastor went on. "We believe this crisis is going to change the way church is done. People will want more relationship and mentorship and to meet in smaller groups, gathering in restaurants and coffee shops. It's all going to change."

I'm not picking on mega-churches. Even smaller churches organize according to the same metrics of attendance and fundraising, and it only continues with the rise of social media likes, shares, and followers.

However, if our measures of success don't work in a crisis, what good are they? Were they ever the right measures of success?

Again, I'm not questioning the motivation of any leader. I know their struggles and frustrations, and with these measures, many want to quit. They feel like a failure. Some have been told they're not called due to a lack of attendance or money.

If numbers alone were the measure of success, Jesus was a failure. A majority of the crowd abandoned him when supporting him was no longer politically expedient. Or he outright offended them (John 6:66). One in his inner circle betrayed him. Many who cried "Hosanna!" yelled "Crucify!" a week later.

> **If our measures of success don't work in a crisis, what good are they?.**

And yet God was pleased with his Son, both before and after his earthly ministry, so much that the Father gave Christ the name above all (Philippians 2:9-11). God considered Jesus a success, the only success.

There's nothing inherently wrong with large meetings. Like all of us, I've gathered with thousands and felt God's presence. I've also sat in a room with a handful of people and known the power of the Spirit. The focus here is to find a universal, transcendent, biblical, and kingdom-minded model.

The administrative pastor I spoke to expressed the conundrum of every church during the lockdowns. How do we teach and encourage people? How do we help people grow in Christ when they're *stuck at home*?

Many churches put everything online. Do the same stuff, only on the internet.

Others had this radical idea. What if this COVID crisis was an opportunity to *send* our people? What if we activated and empowered our congregation to go out and invite their neighbors into their lives and homes?

What if gathering wasn't the right measure? What if it's sending? Would we do Christian life differently?

Many churches are meeting in person again, and most are trying to get the church back to *normal*. But should we? What did we learn? There is now a precedent that governments can shut down gatherings in buildings and send everyone home. We all saw the necessity of empowering the leadership of every believer in their own communities.

For Christians in several countries around the world, these types of restrictions aren't temporary mandates during a pandemic. The inability to gather as believers is an oppressive *normal* for countries hostile to the Gospel. How do Jesus followers measure success in those cultures? In places like China and Iran, churches are growing while the church declines in America. Persecuted believers can't measure success like non-persecuted Christians.

Perhaps we should learn from them. These persecuted disciples spread the Good News, declaring the intimacy and purpose every person desires in their deepest heart. They empower and activate every believer, gathering the reborn as outposts of heaven on earth. They are miraculous living testimonies.

Jesus was the first incarnation, and he revealed the model for how those born of God can live heaven on earth. Since this solution and revolution emanates from the Father, no one can stop it. No government or philosophy or economic system can contain it.

That's what we need to rediscover. The Jesus Model.

Exploration

Identity determines behavior. We act according to what and who we believe we are.

God wants to change our behavior since selfish acts of sin destroy and wound others. God knows the problem with our human nature. Complete transformation of who we are must take place before we can hope to change what we do.

When you think about yourself, who do you believe you are? What defines you? Career? Family role? Personality trait? Sexuality? Failures or flaws? What others think of you?

We are transformed by the renewing of our mind. We must cease identifying ourselves by the temporary. Without God, it is all we have. But with God, we can replace those transient identities with a new, eternal, heavenly one that can't change. God has even given us eternal names.

Father, we are your children, born of heaven. Christ chooses us and we are abundantly and extravagantly loved. We're gifted with a purpose and part of your family. Our lives are hidden in Christ at the right hand of God. That is who we are. Amen.

Chapter 2
The Jesus Model

The United States spearheaded a major invasion into Europe in June 1944. Canadian, Australian, and British forces joined America in the largest military attack in history to push back against Nazi Germany. The Allies trained and planned for months to hit beaches and simultaneously parachute a legion of soldiers behind enemy lines to create havoc in the German military infrastructure.

It was almost a disaster.

Despite the money, power, and overwhelming numbers, plans went awry, especially the soldiers dropping from the sky. Airborne Rangers were scattered miles from their objectives.

One major leadership decision saved D-Day. Every soldier involved in the invasion, from the lowest private to the officers in charge, were taught the entire plan. Every man knew every target, town, road, and hill. They memorized maps and enemy positions. If separated from their unit or platoon, the soldiers had methods to determine friend from foe, link up with others, establish a leader, and choose an objective.

Before the attack, they trained for crisis. Leadership empowered every individual to make the best decision that would have the greatest impact for the sake of the entire mission.

The Germans, however, possessed a different military structure. Enlisted soldiers required orders to act, unable to make decisions apart from their superiors.

During the chaos and confusion that ensued in June 1941, the American soldiers were able to gather, organize, and continue their mission to great success. In contrast, the pandemonium paralyzed the Germans.

The Commission of Jesus

If there is a transcendent and universal model of living heaven on earth, one that applies in every culture and nation, one that finds success in times of plenty and crisis, then we should expect Jesus to have taught us that very model. And, of course, he did.

We all know the commission in Matthew 28. Jesus tells his disciples to go and *make disciples* of every nation, teaching them to obey his commands. As a young man growing up in the church, we repeatedly used this Great Commission in relation to evangelism, which meant, primarily, that we would make converts through a prayer.

Words like evangelism and discipleship trigger mounds of academic definitions and discussions, and subsequent arguments. Let's leave those heady conversations behind for a moment and simply try to take on the perspective of the men to whom Jesus spoke. What would they have heard? *Go make new people like I made new people.*

They walked with Jesus for around three years, saw him minister in powerful ways, heard teachings they didn't understand, and more. The Gospels detail how the disciples lived with Jesus, and considering the ensuing mission to *go make new people like I made new people,* it makes total sense. The writers were, in part, sharing the Jesus Model with us.

Here's what didn't happen for those three years. Jesus didn't invite these men to a class or give them a degree. He didn't make an emotional appeal and count raised hands. He didn't place them in a program with a catchy name, cool graphics, and pumping music. Not that those are inherently bad, but they weren't the Jesus Model.

What did life with Jesus look like?

There was a Gospel, the Gospel of the Kingdom. It was a call for submission and reconciliation with the Father, and to join him in living heaven on earth. This was a specific invitation. No one was coerced or manipulated. The absolute difficulty of the journey was made abundantly clear. They would have to give their whole life (Luke 14:33). Those responding to the call were placed in relationship with a person radically following God, actually and literally God in the flesh, and those followers had mindsets challenged. It taught them about the culture of the Kingdom of Heaven and the love of the Father through relationship, experience, and intimate conversation.

Next, they were given a mission. To go out, take that model, and replicate it with others. But this is a supernatural work, initiated by a man fully human and divine. How can mere humans accomplish this work or replicate it? They can't. Not unless it empowered them with the same ability.

And that's exactly what happened. Jesus said, "I'm sending you as the Father sent me." And then he breathed on them and said, "Receive the Holy Spirit." (John 20:21-22) We must be born again. The supernatural, heavenly birth isn't simply to make us feel good, as much as that can be true with the joy of new birth. Rebirth with the Spirit is a necessary component of the model.

> **We are not normal. We are walking, talking miracles, waiting to be released.**

God placed the Word, his message to all humanity, within a person that walked, healed, spoke truth, and lived among the people he loved.

It didn't stop with Jesus. On the contrary, we now have the Spirit of Jesus walking around in human beings all over the world, millions of them, little atom bombs of love and power going to work and doing normal everyday things.

But we are not normal. We are walking, talking miracles, waiting to be released.

Go and make new people like I made new people. This is the Jesus Model, It shouldn't surprise us because if Jesus came to undo the works of the devil (1 John 3:8) and save that which was lost (Luke 19:10) then make more of you must be part of the redemption.

It was the command we were given at the start.

Go Make More of You

At the very beginning, God designed and established the Garden of Eden, an outpost of heaven on earth. The Father then fashioned a creature out of the dirt, made in God's image, and breathed life into a man.

We all know the story in Genesis of how Adam and Eve ate from the wrong tree and brought corruption and death into the world. They were told to stay away from the Tree of the Knowledge of Good and Evil. But the directive wasn't God's only command.

God gave them intimacy with him and each other, and out of oneness, he gave purpose. Adam's purpose was to spread the Garden of Eden out to the rest of the earth, to take the model of Eden and replicate it. But Adam couldn't spread and manage the Garden by himself. God gave him Eve so they could produce children, the other part of the command. *Be fruitful and multiply.*

To put it another way: God told the people he created in his image to go make more people in his image. They would be one with each other for the express purpose of spreading outposts of heaven across the wilderness of the earth. Intimacy would fulfill the purpose.

By breaking one rule with the wrong tree, Adam and Eve lost access to heaven on earth, including the Tree of Life, and subsequently lost their purpose.

Redemption must include the restoration of purpose. God doesn't do things halfway. In fact, one of God's most amazing qualities is how his redemption always exceeds what was lost, even by our own selfish stupidity, like the example of the best wine at the end of the wedding in Cana (John 2).

The Jesus Model we've been discussing has its roots in God's original design and purpose for humanity. Only now it is through Christ and in a New Covenant. It's bigger and eternal.

The work of the Father in the New Covenant through Jesus gives us Christ (the tree of life), the reborn new creation (made in his likeness), access to the Kingdom of Heaven (the Garden of Eden), and we are to spread the Good News of the Kingdom to all nations (bring the earth under dominion) by bringing more reborn followers into the family of God (be fruitful and multiply).

God not only restores what we lost but lifts us to a greater, spiritual life and mission.

To help us better understand the Jesus Model, I will endeavor to express the Kingdom as he did. Through story.

The Power of Story

Story is powerful. While theology is necessary and important, it alone is complicated and limiting, even divisive and uninviting. Story is complex, allowing deep truths to be expressed in simple ways. Even a short story can reveal eternal, living truths of identity, doctrine, and theology. But a story does more. Narrative connects and gathers people, revealing the longings of our hearts and telling us how truth must be lived to be real.

God not only restores what we lost but lifts us to a greater, spiritual life and mission.

Stories also answer one of the most important questions we ask, often the most difficult. *Why?* When faced with chaos and crisis, it is the first question on our lips and in our hearts. Why is this happening? Stories tell us why.

So why did Jesus come? Why have we been born again?

Jesus always included stories when he taught (Mark 4:34). The Scripture calls them parables. Since he is the model, so should I.

Through the narrative of the resurrection of Lazarus from John 11, we will explore the Jesus Model to bring heaven to earth. We will use this amazing story as a framework and foundation to declare and discuss the deep mysteries of what it means to live as Christ on the earth. We will enter this story together, learning from the Father.

We will divide the story of Lazarus and the Jesus Model into three parts: Roll Away the Stone, Life from the Dead, and Unwrapping the Gift.

As Wendy said in Hook, we will learn to Crow, to Fly, and to Fight.

Before we get begin with Rolling Away the Stone, we must learn Rule #1.

Exploration

Billions, maybe trillions, of dollars have been generated by blockbuster stories like *Star Wars* and *Lord of the Rings*. Each begins with an ordinary person given an extraordinary call to adventure. On what we designate the *hero's journey*, the main character must accept a call. He or she will need to leave their world behind and move forward into an unknown adventure full of wonder, mystery, and terror.

Why do we love these epic stories? Because we were created to be a part of one. This is what God does, inviting us into the most epic story of all as the Father reconciles all creation back to himself through his Son.

The Gospel is a call to adventure within God's story. Just like the heroes in so many epic tales, that is our transformation.

Yet what if Luke stayed on the moisture farm and did not go with Obi Wan? What if Frodo hadn't volunteered to take the ring to Mordor? They would have personally avoided some pain and tragedy, and much inconvenience. But the world would have been worse off, and their own lives still tragic by extension. They wouldn't have avoided pain and grief, only delayed it.

Their acceptance of the call into the larger story changed themselves, saved others, even the world or galaxy.

We also must willingly choose to leave our own lives behind for the eternal adventure. We can't keep our idea of a normal, safe life and have an epic story at the same time. A choice must be made.

What do you choose? Keep reading if you dare.

Father, thank you for inviting us into the greatest story ever told, the one that will echo through eternity. Give us the courage and the strength to leave our lives behind and accept the call. Amen.

Chapter 3
Rule #1: Don't Freak Out

My wife and I visited friends in Tennessee, and they invited us to a huge cookout. I sat down at a table to eat, a toddler in a highchair next to me. He only wore his diaper, and at some point, he accidentally dumped his bowl of Cheerios all over himself.

Covered in milk and cereal, he gasped and stood in the highchair. The child raised his hands and said, "Don't freak out."

My mouth dropped.

The mother appeared and began cleaning him up, and I asked, "Did he say, 'don't freak out'?"

"Oh yeah," she said. "That's rule #1 in our family."

"You have rules?"

She explained the toddler was the youngest of several boys and they had developed three rules. Rule #2 was "no blood, no Band-Aid." Rule #3 was a complicated one about when it was appropriate to laugh when someone falls down.

My wife and I had smaller kids at the time and quickly adopted Rules #1 and #2 in our household. I also follow Rule #1 in my life and teach it to others.

Freaking out is being ruled by fear, reacting out of the crisis and chaos instead of faith. Operating from fear is a poor foundation. Major logic portions of our brain shut down when overwhelmed by fear, and we respond through fight, flight, or freeze.

The Scripture, however, gives us another option. Faith. "Be still and know that I am God." (Psalm 46:10) Only those with the indwelling Holy Spirit have that option. As we discuss the Jesus Model, we must begin where Jesus did in the story of Lazarus—not reacting in fear and chaos but obeying in peace and faith.

Your Friend is Dying

My wife and I were serving in Korea as missionary teachers when I checked my email during a planning break. I had received one from my mother. *I'm so sorry to tell you like this, but Larry Trammell passed away today.*

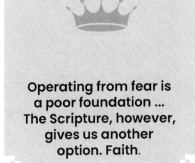

Operating from fear is a poor foundation ... The Scripture, however, gives us another option. Faith.

Larry was a spiritual father to me and my wife. He had shared so much with us from the Spirit, and we were like family with Larry, his wife, and kids. A healthy man and relatively young at 50, his death was a shock.

My wife also taught at the school, and I arranged for her to get coverage for class. Once alone in the hallway, I told her the news, and we wept together for a long time.

What about the funeral? We were a fourteen-hour flight away from Atlanta, where we had lived, and the Trammell family still did. Feeling somewhat hopeless, we called family and friends back in the states, and we struggled with whether to make the trip. My wife and I prayed and felt God tell us to go back for Larry's celebration of life service, despite the expense. We were confident in the decision, and God worked out every detail.

I can easily relate to what Jesus must have felt when he heard his friend Lazarus was dying in John 11. Jesus was close to Lazarus and his two sisters, Mary and Martha.

Jesus didn't react in a way that made sense. Wouldn't he rush and go see him right away? Instead, the Son of God explained the story of Lazarus wouldn't end in death, and all that happened would be to the glory of God.

As much as he loved Lazarus, he trusted the goodness of his Father more. The Father said, "Wait," and so he waited two days. Lazarus died. At that seemingly hopeless point, God said, "Go to Lazarus." Then Jesus moved.

God did more than just tell Jesus what to do. He let him in on the plan. "Lazarus is sick, but it won't end in death ... He's asleep, but I'm going to wake him up."

Intimacy and purpose are inseparable, and yet we begin the journey with intimacy. We are a sent people, and it matters from whom we are sent.

The only activity that lasts into eternity is that which is birthed from walking with God. (1 Corinthians 3:12-13)

Follow Me and I Will ...

There's only one person who fully knows how to live the incarnation. Jesus. The perfect, complete God in human form lived by a simple principle. He only did what he saw the Father do and said what God said (John 5:19; John 12:49). Even sinless, the Son of God didn't trust his own opinions. "For I have come down from heaven to do the will of God who sent me, not to do my own will." (John 6:38)

Those statements require relationship. To hear and see, I must be close enough to listen and look. Everything good and eternal flows from a discipline of relationship with the Father through Christ in the Spirit. Everything.

As Jesus approached a couple of brothers along the shore to invite them into God's story and live heaven on earth, the recruitment and promise was incredibly simple. "Come, follow me, and I will show you how to fish for people!" (Matthew 4:19)

Jesus didn't say read this book, take a class, watch his series of videos, go get a special certificate, or a host of other things. Those may be good, but it's not what he said.

"Follow me, the Son of God. Your job is to cling to me, stick with me, trust me, move with me. I will do the making. That's my job. I will make you an agent of redemption from that actively following relationship."

Larry Trammell had a T-shirt he loved, and he adopted it as a life motto. So have I. "Religion Sucks, Jesus Rules."

The New Testament doesn't speak well of religious traditions. Traditions are symbols without substance and will never be the goal. The substance is in Christ, so the writers of the New Testament continually urge us to be in him. Paul wrote that circumcision and uncircumcision meant nothing; all that mattered was the new creation. (Galatians 6:15)

We like religious traditions because we can control, manipulate, maintain, and take credit for them. Instead, we must adhere to the simplicity in Christ.

Walking step by step with God is unpredictable, mysterious, frightening, and miraculous.

This seems lazy, super mystical, or impractical. The opposite is true. Did Jesus just sit around doing nothing the whole time? No, the one who did and said only what came from his Father was so active that if all that he did was written down, the world couldn't contain the books (John 21:25). We are called to activity, but it is absolutely important where that activity is born—the heart of God or our own efforts?

Walking step by step with God is unpredictable, mysterious, frightening, and miraculous. We can't see the wind, don't know where it comes from or where it's going. Such are the people born of the Spirit (John 3:8). In the life of the born-again, we can't control or maintain life. We definitely can't take credit for it.

Even though the disciples didn't understand why Jesus stayed when he heard Lazarus was sick, or even why he left when he did, they stuck with him. John 11 was toward the end of Jesus's ministry, at the height of conflict with the Jewish religious leadership. It was dangerous to get so close to Jerusalem.

The disciples kept following anyway, despite their lack of understanding, saying, "Come, let's go die with him," due to the danger of the situation. This was only one of the chances the disciples had to quit, turn back, or give up. But if they had, they would have missed the miracle. Walking with God feels uncertain and unpredictable, but it's also the only path where we see miracles.

Religious tradition tempts us because we are seeking security. But as Admiral Ackbar from Star Wars says, "It's a trap!" Doing life in our own strength only leads to more fear and anxiety, not security or peace.

We find the peace we long for by surrendering to God's rule and reign and trusting in his promises and goodness, not in our ability.

Surrendering is often difficult in the middle of the story.

The Middle of the Story

Here's one thing I can guarantee. On this journey with Christ, amazing and joyous as it may be, we will want to quit. Often. How do I know? The Bible tells us several times to endure, to not give up. That means I'll be tempted to quit. And I have. We all have.

Jesus promises we will have trouble and the road of eternal life is difficult (John 16:33). When crisis and chaos overwhelm us, we want to quit.

Watching movies with my kids, the film would get to the *darkest before the dawn* moment. In a well written story, there's a moment when the main character has suffered enough, and they want to quit. It seems hopeless.

I would stop the movie with my kids and say, "Well, that's it. Story's over."

My children would revolt. "Dad! It's not over! We want to see the end!"

Those dark moments in stories resonate with us because we often feel a sense of loss and hopelessness when darkness and chaos enter our lives. Giving up seems easy then.

But it's not the end of the story. There's more ahead. Frodo makes it back to the shire. Luke redeems his father.

Don't treat the middle of the story like the end of the story. A temporary situation doesn't change an eternal truth.

Jesus didn't end with the promise of trouble because that would stink. He continued with, "But don't be afraid because I've overcome the world." Not just the trouble, but the world and the devil and everything that produced the trouble we're dealing with. He overcame it all.

There are more unwavering promises of God. "And we know that God causes everything to work together for the good of those who love God and are called according to his purpose for them. (Romans 8:28) Not half or most, but all things. We know the end of the story, and it gives us the hope we need to endure. All the bad, the tragedy, the chaos, the failures—all are redeemed for those who love God and participate in his purpose.

That's difficult when the chaos and evil appear to be winning. What are the first things we begin to question when death surrounds us? Not surprisingly, it's the love of God and his purpose. Does he love us? Does any of this matter?

Jesus arrives amidst Lazarus' funeral when he arrives in Bethany, where Lazarus lived. It seemed as if death had won.

Mary and Martha both give the same heartbreaking statement. "If you had been here, he wouldn't have died."

I've felt that way. "God, why did you let this happen? I thought you loved me." In my doubt, despair and questioning, God expressed this truth to me. "The story isn't over yet." Even when it seems death and chaos have won. They haven't.

Jesus speaks this truth to Martha. "Your brother will live again."

Martha, who often gets a bad rap, responds with perfect theology. "I know he'll be resurrected on the last day." Later.

Jesus reveals a deeper truth. "I am the resurrection and the life." He is. The person of the Son of God. Resurrection isn't simply a later event. Resurrection is a present and eternal person. Our resurrection later is possible because we are in the One who is the resurrection now.

The world needs to see and hear this truth through us living heaven on earth.

From Rest

The first day that Adam and Eve knew was rest.

God created everything, saving humanity as the best for last, and the very next day, God rested. God does nothing by accident. He purposefully taught them rest and peace before anything else.

He gave them purpose and commands to multiply and fill the earth as we've discussed, but the perfect and complete way, the sinless way, was to work from rest, not to achieve it. Because they couldn't. Eden was a finished work, set up before he created them. They were invited into God's work with him, to have intimacy in his activity.

The curse, however, flipped it. After the Fall, Adam and Eve had to work to survive. Humanity had to earn a rest that didn't last. Working to get rest is the result of brokenness, not wholeness.

God wants to return us to being whole and complete in him, so he gives an eternal rest back to us in Christ and the Kingdom. We can now move forward in our purpose from God's rest. It is his, not ours, which means it is stable and secure. We are a part of, and inheriting, an unshakable Kingdom, a finished work we choose to participate in.

Jesus makes this point in Matthew 6. Unbelievers worry about what to eat or what to wear. The redemption is our call to seek first the Kingdom and provision for our need supernaturally follows. Because God cares for us and loves us more than we can imagine, he wants us to walk with him in his purpose without fear, anxiety, or insecurity. Our abilities and the things of this world can't give us what we desire.

Now we can share peace and rest—the Hebrew *shalom* of complete wholeness. He keeps us in perfect shalom when we set our minds on him. Jesus gives a peace the world has no power to provide.

In Philippians 4, Paul tells us not to worry. Well, that helps. Have you ever told someone not to worry or calm down? Rarely works. But Paul doesn't stop there. He describes the secret and function of prayer. Tell God what we need. Believe he loves us. Be thankful for what he's done. *Then* the peace of God will guard our heart and mind as we live in Christ. The shalom we long for results from choosing to walk with Christ and lift our attention on who he is, what he's done, and what he's promised he will do.

We can't help our first initial emotional reaction; the temptation to *freak out* is real. With the power of Christ, I now have the option of taking captive those thoughts and redirecting my focus to the all-powerful Father who loves me.

Then I will experience peace. And with peace, I can bring hope and peace to the suffering of others. This is the purpose of God.

And the purpose of God is born of love.

Exploration

"Martha," Jesus said, "you are worried about many things, but only one thing is needed. Mary has chosen that thing."

Awkward. Sisters don't like being compared, but Martha started it, pulling Jesus aside to make him tell Mary to help with the practical things. Jesus corrects her. "Watch Mary. She's chosen what's better."

Martha thought she had to get everything done before she could be at rest. Mary chose to start at peace and rest at the feet of Jesus.

If Jesus had told Mary to make him a sandwich, she would have popped up from the floor and started working. The gift is that she would have done it from rest, joy, and peace in relationship instead of her own power.

Choose each day to find rest in Christ first, before any activity of your day. This will keep you grounded and secure as you face what is ahead.

Father, thank you for your mercy and love. Thank you for your provision and the gifts you've given us. We trust you with our needs and the situations we care about. Keep us close to you and give us the strength to stay with you in all t

ONE

CROW

Roll Away the Stone

When Jesus saw her weeping and saw the other people wailing with her, a deep anger welled up within him, and he was deeply troubled. "Where have you put him?" he asked them.

They told him, "Lord, come and see." Then Jesus wept. The people who were standing nearby said, "See how much he loved him!" But some said, "This man healed a blind man. Couldn't he have kept Lazarus from dying?"

Jesus was still angry as he arrived at the tomb, a cave with a stone rolled across its entrance. "Roll the stone aside," Jesus told them.

But Martha, the dead man's sister, protested, "Lord, he has been dead for four days. The smell will be terrible."

Jesus responded, "Didn't I tell you that you would see God's glory if you believe?"

(John 11:33-40)

The first step in the Jesus Model is to *roll away the stone.*

Rolling away the stone removes all the obstacles between the spiritually dead and the only source of life—the Lord Jesus Christ.

Rolling away the stone is essentially learning how to crow. To crow is to preach the Gospel of the Kingdom through word and deed. We don't discuss the Kingdom; we declare it. Rolling away the stone enters the mess of a broken and dying world to reveal the truth of a realm people long for but believe impossible. It is shows a realm of love, immortality, purpose, and deep intimacy with a Father who abundantly loves them. A place of joy and hope and peace. The Father is inviting them to that place, calling their name through Jesus.

The stone symbolizes all that stands between people and their encountering salvation through Christ. The stone represents the lies they believe, the wounds they carry, the selfishness that blinds them and leads them down paths of destruction.

In the Scripture, Jesus didn't roll away the stone. He could have, surely, with a simple command. But he didn't.

He gave that task to people. Not one singular person but a community who had also shown up to grieve with Mary and Martha. Why give it to people?

Humanity placed the stone there. Literally, in John 11, men had rolled the stone in place over the grave before Jesus arrived. Humanity also began participating in the lie from Adam and Eve onward, bringing death and destruction into God's perfect design. We cling to the stone, erecting it as some sort of safeguard and security. However, all it does is keep us in the dark and separate from the God who loves us.

Our redemption, therefore, is to take part in removing the very barriers we helped to erect. We couldn't start that process, which is why Jesus came in the flesh to show us how to do it. He trained men that would then train others who would ... you get the idea.

The first aspect of the Jesus Model. We must learn to CROW, to Roll Away the Stone.

Chapter 4
Nothing but Love

Everyone talks about love. The Beatles told us, "All you need is love." People fall in love, tumble back out, and often back in again. The topic dominates most popular music, and the romance genre is one of the most lucrative in publishing. I can love my kids, a woman, or several, or an ice cream cone and my car.

The word *love* is used so indiscriminately it has lost meaning. While we enjoy coming up with our own definitions, the self-defining path hasn't led to more security, contentment, or gotten us closer to a world that is inherently good. The shifting sand of modern sacred subjectivity has brought us more division, destruction, self-destruction, hate, fear, and anxiety.

Fortunately, God hasn't left us in this morass without a way forward. The one who designed this world and created our very beings knows all and reveals what we need to know.

Love isn't a standard apart from God. We go terribly wrong when we feel love is separate from the person of God, as if we can judge God's actions according to our limited ability to understand. God is love (1 John 4:8). His nature is love. When he acts and decides, those choices are the definition of love.

God is a being wholly apart from us, someone whose ways are not our ways and thoughts aren't our thoughts. There is a gap between Creator and the fallen creation where we have no way of even knowing or experiencing genuine love. This is epically tragic, since it is what we desperately desire. Our obsession with love is evident even as we butcher it with our own misunderstanding.

The love of heaven is so beyond us, the apostle Paul had to appropriate a rarely used Greek word, *agape*, to describe the heavenly truth of love. His beautiful description in 1 Corinthians 13 comes down to this: *Love is acting according to the eternal best for everyone.* Love is doing what God would do in a situation. He tells us what to do, since he knows the full impact of every decision.

God couldn't just leave us with the wrong idea of love. He had to make a way. To reveal that he himself is true love, he had to be the example, hence the incarnation. God entered the broken story of this world. He felt our pain and was tempted in every way (Hebrews 4:15), lived every tragedy of betrayal and grief we could possibly experience. Yet he revealed how love should act and respond. He showed us what love looks like among hate and pain.

During his life, he was limited to one God-person. How could he touch every life? He couldn't. He placed the person of love, the Holy Spirit, within others and now spreads more examples of God's love through you and me. Not only writing or speaking about love but also living love out loud in front of a people in desperate need of a different example than culture, entertainment, philosophy, education, and the authorities of this world have given them.

Love was God's motivation ...For us to engage anyone in truth, it must also be ours.

If we don't start and continue in God's love, nothing we do matters. The love of God in our hearts is the only foundation for engaging the world to remove the barriers between humanity and God. The people in John 11 only acted by the command of Christ, and we can't forget that we move forward with him, listening to his voice and responding.

Love was God's motivation. "For God so loved the world …" For us to engage anyone in truth, it must also be ours.

See How He Loved Him

Jesus didn't invite Lazarus to the synagogue.

That sounds ridiculous, but the dead aren't coming to our meetings. They're dead. They're out there locked away behind whatever form their barriers take. We must go to them.

Jesus went to the funeral. Funerals aren't fun. In fact, they can be chaotic and messy. Emotions like anger, fear, and hopelessness accompany the experience of grief. This is the scene Jesus enters, and he deals with questions and doubts from family and friends of Lazarus.

Of course. the very truth of Jesus leaving heaven for earth shows his willingness to enter our brokenness and confusion. Jesus showing up to the funeral is only one of many examples we have.

However, he didn't simply show up. Twice, Jesus also expresses deep emotion, weeping, angry, groaning. He expressed a grief so evident people said, "See how he loved Lazarus!"

Hold on a minute. Why did he weep if Lazarus would live again?

Two reasons. First, God never dismisses pain. Yes, he redeems and makes all things new, but that doesn't mean the abuses of life don't hurt. God not only acknowledges the pain, he weeps with us in our pain. The Scripture clearly calls us to weep with those who weep and rejoice with those who rejoice (Romans 12:15), living with people and relating to them in their circumstances. Because we love them. Because that's compassion.

Second, and connected, I believe Jesus was angry at death. He was angry at sin, at destruction, at the perversion of his Father's creation that culminates in the grief of death.

Before COVID, my family went to serve Christmas breakfast at the Atlanta Mission for several years with our church family. I went the first year, took my 7-year-old son the next. This service opportunity required us to wake up at 4am and drive downtown. The first time my son went, he imagined having fun with other kids, like he did on Sundays, and he was disappointed to learn we were there to work. I explained to him we were cooking and serving for a group of homeless men that would soon arrive.

"After we're done here," I said, "you and I will go back and be with our family and open presents and have an amazing Christmas. These men will go back out on the street, and most of them either don't have families or the ones they have don't talk to them. We're going to love them and give them a good Christmas breakfast."

That 7-year-old boy pulled it together and did a phenomenal job pouring syrup over blueberry pancakes.

A great deal of people come to serve with us, and there aren't enough *jobs* for everyone to cook or take food out to the tables. That's by design. Pastor Brian Holland makes it clear that the most important action is look these men in the eye, ask their names, and engage them in conversation. Ask for their stories. Listen. Dignify them as human beings.

My son was young enough to take that to heart. Once all the food had been served, he sat across from a rough-looking gentleman and introduced himself with a smile. My son was an example to us all that day.

It's Gonna Stink

Jesus told people to roll away the stone, and Martha responded, "Uh, Jesus. Not sure if you know this, but Lazarus has been dead for four days. It's gonna be kinda rank in there."

He answered her, "Didn't I tell you that if you believed, you'd see the glory of God? Roll away the stone."

How will we see resurrections if we don't go where dead people are?

We are sent to the spiritually dead of this world, and dead people *stink*. They have problems. They're messy. They make bad choices, say hurtful things. Sometimes, they aren't so fun to be around.

This never stopped Jesus. He dealt with lepers and those the Jews considered unclean, one of the major criticisms of the religious–he eats with sinners! (Mark 2:16-17) Thank God, because we were once dead, too.

Yep. Jesus explains he came for this purpose. He came for the lost and the hurting. We are chosen by God and born again from heaven for the same purpose and motivation.

At the Atlanta Mission, they accept many into an addiction recovery program. It is a great program, which we support, but there are issues. Addiction recovery is fraught with failures. We risk relationships with men and women that could relapse at any point or take advantage of our kindness, steal, lie, cheat, and more. And yes, they also don't always have the best hygiene.

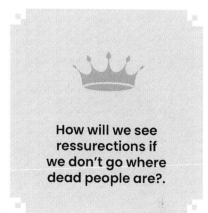

How will we see ressurections if we don't go where dead people are?.

We don't seek to dignify and love these men who deal with addiction because it's easy or fun or because it's 100% effective. There are disappointments and tragedies. We choose to get involved because we love them. Because they are worth it.

They have eternal value. They are made, fashioned carefully, fearfully, and wonderfully, by God. Created in his image.

The men at the Atlanta Mission are just one example. We could list a host of other legitimate ways to bring dignified relief to the broken and hurting. In each instance, we engage and enter the pain of others because these are people with eternal value and are worthy of the dignity and love from the heart of God.

Grief and the Kingdom of Heaven

We all know, deep in our beings, the world around us isn't how it should be.

Death is common in our world. It is inevitable. This is called entropy. Things deteriorate and die. No matter how much we build, one day it will be destroyed. No matter how hard we work to eat or be healthy, we will die. It's inescapable. Hopeless.

If death is the way of life, then why does it upset us? Why do we grieve at all?

Because we weren't created to lose one another.

The original design didn't include death. We brought that in, believing the lies of the Devil. Believing the lies of the enemy always leads to death. God's truth leads to life.

The lie is God must not exist since there is death. God doesn't know; or if he knows, he just doesn't care. None of those are true.

The truth is revealed in Jesus at the grave. He wept. He grieves with us.

Grief is an expression of the Kingdom. Our grief makes the statement, "It's not supposed to be like this." We may not know why we feel that way, but we do.

God agrees with us.

Modern western Christianity hasn't done a bang-up job teaching people how to grieve well. Grief is messy and uncomfortable. Parties and worship concerts are much more fun. God, who is love, grieves for us and with us. We do the people of God a disservice by not teaching each another to weep for what makes God weep and to lament the pain of this world.

There is a complete book of the Bible called Lamentations, by the way.

When we grieve with people, we agree with them. *This isn't the way life is supposed to be.* God agrees, too. We long for a different life because it exists. That life is called the Kingdom of God.

One of my favorite definitions of the Kingdom of God is, "Life as God created it to be." People weren't meant to get sick, die, hurt each other, hate each other, kill, steal, rape, and more. That wasn't his plan.

The Good News of the Gospel is the Kingdom is both here and on its way. The world we long for exists and we can be a part of it. The Gospel of the Kingdom expresses the truth that God is setting things right. We must change our way of thinking, being, and doing to that eternal reality. The Kingdom is arriving. Heaven is coming to earth. Repent. Turn to God and join him by living heaven on earth now.

We preach this Kingdom with words, absolutely, but our actions must align with those words. Speaking alone can't reveal the Kingdom because words of declaration, while necessary, are limited. God, by his very nature, over fulfills all his promises because the eternal can't be properly expressed within a statement of human language.

Like the parables of Jesus, stories are complex and can reveal eternal truths in a way theological or doctrinal statements are unable. Therefore, preaching the Gospel also happens through living that story, living according to the principles of heavenly reality, and choosing to participate in righting the wrongs we see around us, whether in our household, at our jobs, in our community, nation, or the world. All of it.

That's love. Not only to speak what is true, but also to live accordingly. We need both.

Exploration

What does it mean to love our neighbor?

When asked this question, Jesus responded with a story. We call it the story of the Good Samaritan (Luke 10:25-37). A man, a Jew, is attacked while on a journey and left for dead. Two religious Jews pass him by, refusing to stop and help him.

But Jesus chose the third man to reveal complete and perfect love. This man was a Samaritan, someone the Jews would have considered an unclean half-breed, and a religious heretic. Yet this racial and religious *other* was the one who acted out of love.

What did he do? He saw, had compassion, placed himself in danger and risk, and took his own time and money to minister to the man left for dead.

Even better, look at what he didn't do. He didn't pass by like the religious. He didn't decide to vote for a political party that would act for him or protest to the political and religious authorities to add more security on the road. He didn't post on social media about how sad it was. He didn't tell his pastor how someone needed to do something.

The Samaritan took responsibility himself. His love cost him something—time, security, money. The Samaritan acted as Jesus did, to see the pain, have compassion, enter the pain, and act to make it right. That's loving our neighbor as ourselves.

It will be the same with you. How are you personally involved with others? How are you giving of yourself to love those in your sphere of life and influence?

Father, open our eyes to the pain surrounding us, those that are hurting and need your love and hope. Give us your love and compassion to act for healing, righteousness, and justice. Amen.

Chapter 5
Redemptive Justice

"Touch that and I'll smack you!"

When dealing with our three children, my wife has a list of statements we never thought we'd have to say to our kids. "Don't lick that!" "Why did you put that in your ear?"

Kids get angry at each other. They are little humans and begin to understand ownership and right and wrong at a very young age. A toddler will find something they like and will announce to everyone, "This is mine!" Doesn't matter if it belongs to them or not, it's theirs because they want it. When another child comes to claim it, the toddler will feel wronged. And then the fight breaks out.

As parents, we guide our children along the way, in part to keep them from hitting or biting another kid. One of our three was a biter. Sharing is a value we try to pass on, setting up play dates and placing them in preschool where the word *share* is frequently said and taught.

Children develop a sense of justice, too, very early. Depending on the kid, they will respond in different ways to a felt injustice. Some will cry or tattle or both, trying to appeal to a higher authority like an adult. Others start swinging, ready to assert their authority and mete out justice by their own hand like a vigilante. Those are punitive forms of justice.

Our adult world isn't very different. It might sound harsh, but though the years pass and the tools change, we mature little. The justice of the world is largely based on punitive measures. The *eye for an eye* principle.

Punitive justice doesn't work, though. Most of us probably support putting a criminal in jail, but the statistics are clear—prison doesn't rehabilitate very well. In fact, looking at rates of recidivism (from 30% up to 70% in some states), prison can create harder, lifelong criminals.

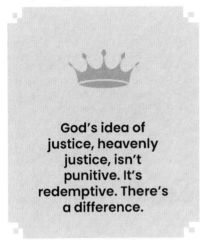

God's idea of justice, heavenly justice, isn't punitive. It's redemptive. There's a difference.

I'm not arguing against prison or even punishment, but that's all the world has to offer. Behavior modification only goes so far, and if the New Testament tells us anything, we know the regulations and the requirements of the law saved nothing. No hearts were changed. Laws only told us how wrong we were and taught us more ways to do bad. We needed a different way. A different law. (Romans 4:15)

God's idea of justice, heavenly justice, isn't punitive. It's redemptive. There's a difference.

Writers of the New Testament had a unique and phenomenal example of what redemptive justice looked like, a national symbol of God's heart for restoration.

The Year of Jubilee

The Old Testament gets a bad rap sometimes. In Exodus 21, we read, "An eye for an eye and a tooth for a tooth." Gandhi rightly stated, "An eye for an eye leaves the whole world blind." But that's not the end of that statement from Exodus 21, though. To end it there is incomplete. The next phrase: "But vengeance is mine says the Lord."

It is a godly thing to long for justice, for situations and circumstances to be set right, and yet our understanding of what needs to happen, and even what is wrong, is limited at best. We simply can't and don't know everything, every motivation, every story, and therefore can't decide in the best interest of every person.

God does. And while God states that to hurt my neighbor, to steal, kill or commit adultery, is wrong, God knows those actions are symptoms of a deeper injustice—a corrupt and broken world influenced by our sinful natures and the lies and influence of the Devil.

Remember, Jesus came to *seek and save that which was lost* and to *undo the works of the Devil*. Those aren't disconnected statements. They're the same. Undoing the curse and the work of the Devil will cause the ending of the symptoms and actions that follow—murder, racism, greed, and all of it. That's God's idea of justice.

God gave the Old Testament law, while insufficient for salvation, to lead us to Jesus. Within the ceremonial symbolism of the law, we see hints of the substance we have in Christ.

One example is the Year of Jubilee. (Leviticus 25)

Upon reaching the Promised Land, God divided the real estate through Joshua for the tribes and priests to inhabit. Tribes with more population received more land, those with less population received land. God gave families parcels according to their size. This was a holy and sacred design. So sacred it was a sin to move a boundary marker. (Deuteronomy 19:14)

People make mistakes, though. Stuff happens. Over time, families lost their land to tragedy or their own dumb decisions. People had to sell themselves into slavery to survive.

The division of land by God wasn't a suggestion. It was a design from heaven.

Therefore, God instituted the Year of Jubilee. Every fifty years, everything went into a big reset. Everyone could reclaim their land. All slaves were set free. Everything went back to how God intended it. All in one fell swoop.

Other laws surrounded Jubilee. If you sold or bought land, the value was determined by the number of years left until the next Jubilee. For instance, if there were forty years left, you paid most of the value, knowing you'd get more out of it over time. If only five years were left of the fifty, then you bought for a small amount since the land would revert to the original owner soon. The same type of rules applied to slaves.

This happened on a national scale. For all tribes. All the people of Israel.

This is redemptive justice. This is God's heart.

Notable Elements of the Jubilee

The simple grace and mercy of the event is initially overwhelming. It didn't matter what they did, why they did it, or if everyone thought they suffered enough. Their land was going to be restored. Consequences of painful decisions or trauma occurred in the meantime, but the restoration was coming, and people didn't have to deserve it.

Second, the Jubilee would have been a constant event in their thinking— a hopeful reality hovering over people and their neighbors. The Jubilee reminded them of God's generosity and love. A neighbor might be poor today, but he and his family would one day be restored to his part of the inheritance within the promise.

Third, all were equal under the Jubilee. Slavery, power over another, wasn't part of the promise because it wasn't part of God's heavenly economy. It was eliminated every fifty years.

The Kingdom of Heaven isn't about coercion or manipulation or force, only consent, which keeps it flowing in love.

Fourth, the Jubilee wasn't for the entire world but singularly for those who lived within the boundaries of the kingdom of Israel, for those he chose as his people. To be sure, a prosperous Israel also blessed the other people groups around them, but the Jubilee was for those in covenant with God.

Fifth, it only worked according to the consent of both individuals and the whole. While the law provided leadership in the form of judges and priests, and a deliverer when needed, there was no central government as we would understand it. There definitely wasn't an institution powerful enough to enforce such a sweeping and universal event. The whole population had to agree to give property back and release slaves. The Kingdom of Heaven isn't about coercion, manipulation, or force, only consent, which keeps it flowing in love.

Later, under David, Solomon, and other kings, a central government with a standing army existed, but the history of that system is a lesson in failure of the power of humanity. The request for a king was considered a great sin, even though God used that rebellion to bring about the truth that God is the only king.

Sixth, people were allowed to mess it up. At the first settling of the promised land and then at every subsequent Jubilee, the nation redeemed what was lost and re-instituted God's heavenly plan. A couple of days after the Jubilee, I'm assuming, somebody messed up. It probably didn't take long, and they were allowed to make mistakes. The same consent and choice that brought the blessing also allowed for major foul-ups.

In other words, they didn't and couldn't force some utopia on earth. As noble as those attempts may be through various misguided forms of government, they always fail because they require worldly force to accomplish it. This is only another form of slavery. The Kingdom is eternal and of a whole other world and slavery has no part. Israel in the Promised Land, the Tabernacle, Temple, David's Jerusalem, and even the Church, both universal and local, were and are all meant to be declarations on earth of another, far better and eternal country.

In John 11, Lazarus rose from the dead, and yet he died again later, as far as we know. He came waddling out of that grave, but he wasn't immortal. His resurrection was only a symbol and sign of the greater one to come.

The Jubilee in the Jesus Model

Did Jesus operate according to the idea of the Jubilee? Obviously the answer is a huge *yes*.

Jesus stands up in the synagogue and reads from Isaiah 61. "The Spirit of the Lord is upon me, for he has anointed me to bring Good News to the poor. He has sent me to proclaim that captives will be released, that the blind will see, that the oppressed will be set free, and that the time of the Lord's favor has come." He rolled up the scroll, handed it back to the attendant, and sat down. All eyes in the synagogue looked at him intently. Then he began to speak to them. "The Scripture you've just heard has been fulfilled this very day!" (Luke 4:18-21)

John the Baptist sent his disciples to ask if Jesus was the Messiah (Matthew 11). The Son of God responded, "Go back to John and tell him what you have heard and seen— the blind see, the lame walk, those with leprosy are cured, the deaf hear, the dead are raised to life, and the Good News is being preached to the poor."

Both are examples of how Jesus clearly worked to redeem what was lost, all according to the revelation of the Kingdom of Heaven. No one is blind, deaf, dead, or sick in the Kingdom. No one is poor or oppressed there.

Jesus preached people should repent because God was going to set everything right. He also gave miraculous signs, reinforcing that reality. *You want to believe the perfect Kingdom of God is arriving? Watch God heal this blind man. Watch me feed the hungry and clothe the naked. Watch me empower people in every interaction. Watch the lame stand up and start dancing. It's happening.*

Jesus didn't require a religious or political position to do any miracles. He was already the Son of God, High Priest, and Eternal King. An earthly crown would have cheapened what he did.

Redemptive Justice Today

The Spirit and the power of God haven't changed in two thousand years. Neither has the model. Acting according to the revelation of the Kingdom of God preaches the reality that there is another world, an invisible and transcendent one. Giving and healing are visible manifestations of what is already true in the unseen.

In God's Kingdom, kids aren't trafficked for sex. Racism and supremacy of one group over another doesn't exist. Hate and division can't be found there. Babies aren't killed. All are equal in value and love.

When we seek to right these wrongs out of compassion and love, and out of a spiritual revelation of what heaven is like, that blessing is for everyone.

One of my favorite speeches by Dr. Martin Luther King, Jr. was about being *maladjusted*. He explained yes, the term refers to a psychological problem, but he declared there are some things to which we should be *maladjusted*. We shouldn't count racism and hate as normal, as was so prominent during his day. If we are adjusted to the culture of heaven, then what is not of the Kingdom must make us weep and act on behalf of others.

Jesus offended many when he acted according to the culture of heaven and against social norms, but it didn't stop him. There were people with desperate needs. In fact, John connects the raising of Lazarus with the later plot of the religious leaders to kill Jesus. (John 11:45-53)

We may not be able to change the government for the better. Although we should desire a good government for the peace of all people, we may only enrage the forces of this world. Anger happens when you declare a transcendent Kingdom to the empires of this earth that seek to maintain their power. Our power and calling are from something and someone far greater (1 John 4:4). Walk in conjunction with the Spirit to treat others according to the culture of heaven, to right what wrongs we can under the Lordship of Christ, and we will live a story that may not make the news but will be put on the big screen in the next life.

Exploration

Do you want to be close to Jesus? He's told us where he is. Serving others.

One of Jesus's parables dealt with the division of the sheep and goats (Matthew 25:31-46). Basically, we don't want to be a goat. But the difference wasn't whether they knew who Jesus was. Both even called him *Lord*. The distinction between them was service to others.

The sheep fed the hungry, clothed the naked, and visited those in prison. They gave their own possessions out of compassion to those that couldn't give back. Jesus equated such service as if they did it to him, personally. The goats were blind to the amazing, eternal opportunity available in serving those in need.

Jesus came to serve, not to be served. You will find him in places serving others out of compassion and expecting nothing in return from them. Go there.

Father, open our eyes to the opportunities to serve around us, from the simple to the extravagant. Give us the humility and the faith to know that we should love and serve, expecting nothing from others because your reward is with you. Amen.

Chapter 6
Unity

The stone between Jesus and Lazarus was so large, it took a community of people to roll it away. No one could have done it alone.

One of my favorite shows as a kid was Voltron. Five friends piloted five mechanical lions. They ran around and flew in space. Voltron was the Defender of the Universe—sounds like a big job.

Every episode used this formula. The bad guys had a witch that would concoct a huge robo-beast monster thing and set it loose against citizens of a planet somewhere. The pilots would be called and zoom away in their lions to fight the beast.

The beast was always too monstrous for them to handle as five individuals. Every episode they had to figure this out, by the way. Eventually, the episode would lead to what every kid was waiting for—the five lions coming together into one humongous robot resembling a human warrior. The leader would say, "Form Voltron!" Then the big, unified robot would get the powerful sword and cut the robo-beast in half with an accompanying explosion and Voltron would save the day.

Until the next episode, when another robo-beast attacked.

As a kid, I always wondered, why didn't they just start unified? Why did they take time fighting as individuals? Just go big, baby. We all knew joining together would happen anyway.

We can laugh at the plot device, but we do the same. We all know we should be unified and not divided.

Before his death, Jesus even expressed that our love for one another would show the world we belonged to him (John 13:35). Not our politics, religious traditions, intellectual or emotional appeals. Loving one another as Christ loved us rolls away the stone and reveals Christ.

That's powerful. Like Voltron times a billion.

I once read Sun Tzu's *Art of War* and realized the ancient book gave us the Devil's playbook. Sun Tzu taught a good military general used division, deception, discouragement, and disruption as tools to weaken the enemy, and cause them to surrender. A face-to-face battle was a failure for a general. Too many situations could go wrong. Division is a far better strategy.

It's also no secret why the Church doesn't participate in unity as it should. We have three enemies according to Scripture: the Devil, human nature, and the systems of the world, and they are doing all they can to divide and disrupt. Different church organizations are called denominations, a term of division. We have thousands of them in the US alone. The last thing the Devil wants is a unified Church.

If the men that set out to roll away the stone from Lazarus's grave had spent their time pushing each other around and arguing over who was the chairman of the *roll away the stone committee*, Lazarus would have never stood up and walked out. Their cooperation was a necessary part of the process.

It wasn't about who was going to get the credit or the title. The point was doing what Jesus wanted them to do. Together. United. To bring life to the dead.

The Desire of the Father

My wife and I have three kids, a son and two daughters. No one prepared me for the feelings of pride and joy when I see my children love each other. Simple acts of kindness or incredibly generous ones generate strong feelings in me to the point I often tell myself to *hold it together, man.*

To be fair, I don't know if anyone could have prepared me. I knew of this phenomenon on some level from other parents, but it is something we must experience on our own to really understand it. True understanding goes deeper than words can express.

The Apostle John writes, " I could have no greater joy than to hear that my children are following the truth." (3 John 1:4) This verse now takes on more meaning to me as a father and as someone who has been a spiritual leader to others.

John was speaking about his spiritual children, not physical. Children and marriage can be a blessing when it is of God, but we can have the same fulfillment (if not more) with those we spiritually lead. To see them grow in their callings and gifts and to speak and walk in truth … there's nothing like it. I get it. No greater joy.

Nothing in this world compares. It's worth the heartache and the struggle and the mess. For those few that latch on and hold tight to the heart of God for themselves and others, my heart bursts with joy.

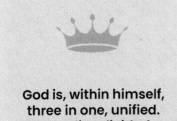

Part of walking in truth is to love one another, to live as one being, each of us members of the Body of Christ (1 Corinthians 12:12). United like a big heavenly Voltron—with two or with millions. God is, within himself, three in one, unified. When we live divided, we lie to the world about the God we serve.

> God is, within himself, three in one, unified. When we live divided, we lie to the world about the God we serve.

Jesus expressed the desire for oneness in his prayer in John 17, where he prays both for the eleven disciples around him and for all who would believe in the future. "I pray that they will all be one, just as you and I are one—as you are in me, Father, and I am in you. And may they be in us *so that the world will believe you sent me.*" Our unity was the prayer of the Lord Jesus Christ, a plea from the Son to the Father through the Spirit, which makes this an eternal longing of the Father that cannot and has not changed in two thousand years.

It was part of the original design. There was one *problem* with the Garden of Eden even before the fall. Adam didn't have anyone like him with whom to commune. Adam didn't point this out to God, by the way. He didn't express any unhappiness or loneliness. God noticed it and provided the solution in another person made in God's image and yet different. Eve.

Living out our oneness in Christ satisfies our own longings for intimacy and purpose, makes our Father happy, and reveals heaven to the world.

As with any work of God, it is not something we can accomplish on our own.

Unity as an Eternal Reality

We can't answer that prayer. We can't make ourselves united any more than we can achieve our own salvation.

The work is done in Christ—where we are already one. The curse of Adam is to work the land to survive and still die, anyway. The gift of the Gospel is that the work is done. We must actively walk in that finished reality, the Kingdom.

We give from wealth, not to gain it. We love from love. We fight from victory. We work from rest. We are able to act unified because we already are one.

To try to achieve *oneness* is chasing our tail. We'll never live it out unless we shift our thinking and rest in what God has done in Christ.

Paul tells us that Christ put to death what divided Jew and Gentile (that's all people) within himself on the cross (Ephesians 2:16). All enmity and division were removed in Christ—me against God, me against myself in the flesh, me against the environment, me against my neighbor, and me against the world. I could not have done what Christ did. No group of people could be big enough or powerful enough to build a tower of Babel that high, because we'd be using worldly means to overcome the world. That doesn't work.

It can only be accomplished by God. Jesus prayed to his Father for it. The Father accomplished it in Christ, and we go to Christ to get it.

Our failure to act as one has its root in our lack of spiritual revelation of the culture of the Kingdom of God. We can't live out in power what we don't see by faith. There's no division in him. Once we understand that, believe and trust it, we can align with what is already true with our brothers and sisters, and have the *experience* of God's oneness.

We aren't talking about simply being nice and tolerating each other. The Scripture speaks of a unity under a higher, transcendent kingdom, one that affirms and corrects every culture, every person. Unity will challenge every race, ethnic group, political perspective, and culture, calling all of us up to something greater and far better. That's the prophetic role of the Church, but we can't do it divided.

The unity and diversity we long for are there together in the Kingdom culture. There are absolutes that are non-negotiable—the Gospel of the kingdom, the person of Christ—and the Scripture makes the non-negotiables clear. For other matters, especially many cultural ones, there is freedom and grace. The old quote from the Lutheran theologian Meldenius serves well: "In essentials, unity; in non-essentials, liberty; in all things, charity."

Just as we need God to do the work of unity, we require his guidance and help to live unity out.

What Divides the World

The divisions of our world seem to have deepened over the past few years. There have always been differences, and yet those differences have taken on greater emotional power in the US and around the world. Political and cultural discourse has continued to devolve between conservative and liberal, Republican and Democrat, as an American example.

There are a host of topics surrounding those political lines, and a central one has been racial unrest, which isn't completely unique to the US. Ethnic and cultural conflict is as old as history itself, one people group seeking dominance over another, fighting over limited resources or other reasons. What is unique in the West is White Supremacy, which developed to justify slavery and discriminatory laws and practices over centuries, codifying that a person is less or more of a person based on the simple color of their skin. Most or all of these laws have been changed, but mentalities and divisions endure.

In addition, disagreement on an issue is now tantamount to hate, and people are *canceled* if the wrong phrase is said or there is even a perceived slight in certain circles. Social media, which has some stated goal of bringing people together, has had the exact opposite effect through click bait titles and digital shouting apart from real relationship. Major corporations make money off our division and hate for one another, causing any conversation or possibly healthy discussion between people to be shut down.

God's not against tribes, people groups, by the way. He's just against using their existence to justify hate, killing, or racism. Israel was a collection of tribes, and even though they all came from Jacob, Isaac, and Abraham, their only hope of unity was in surrendering to the kingship of God.

Even though God has removed and violently obliterated the enmity in the world, these divisions infect the church. As MLK, Jr. famously pointed out, Sunday morning is still one of the most segregated times of the week. This isn't new. The first divisive issue in the book of Acts was when the Greek widows complained about discrimination. The apostles had the people identify leaders in the Church to address it, Barnabas among them (Acts 6:1-4). Ethnic and cultural issues have been a tragic part of the history of the church, as well.

The topics of hate and race are important discussions, but the only hope is to have those in love and relationship, with the heart of God, seeing the *other* as humans loved and created in God's image. Individual issues have value, but we must also realize we're dealing with something much deeper, the Devil's strategy to divide, distract, and destroy. Like the famous quote in *The Usual Suspects*, "The greatest trick the devil ever pulled was to convince the world he didn't exist."

If the greatest power is when the lions join forces to make Voltron, the enemy should do all he can to keep that from happening. And he does.

We must recognize the centrality of Christ and the supremacy and transcendent power of the Kingdom because that's where our unity already exists. That's where it has power.

The Power of Unity

The Bible has some amazing statements regarding God's unity.

The greatest blessing is found in unity. So much of our modern philosophy and culture tries to manufacture unity and diversity, which is a noble endeavor, but it can't happen apart from submission to Christ and the Father. That's where the combined goal of unity and diversity is realized.

Psalm 133 expresses the blessing as the anointing of oil upon the head of the High Priest. Anointing speaks of greater power in the Spirit, all due to us participating in the unity in Christ. Blessing upon blessing, to us and flowing out to others.

Acting in unity with other reborn people in the Spirit has world shaking power. One follower of God can beat a thousand enemies, and yet two will rout ten thousand (Deuteronomy 30:30-32). The effect is not double but exponential. Jesus taught when two or more believers agree, it will be done (Matthew 18:19). By participating in the heart of God in unity, we will live in the miraculous.

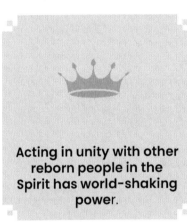

Acting in unity with other reborn people in the Spirit has world-shaking power.

Finally, since loving and free unity and diversity is impossible in our own strength, when it happens in Christ, the world will see we are from another world, a supernatural one, and they will recognize Jesus was sent from the Father. God is three in one, and when we operate in loving unity, people see God. The Gospel is clear and powerful.

To participate in heavenly unity that already exists, loving one another as Jesus, we will have to reach out and listen to believers of different cultures and contexts. We need to be willing to listen and learn from them as gifts of God—all of us humbly laying down our own agendas in submission to the Lord and one another. We may even have to ask or extend forgiveness, or both, to reconcile in God's love and be the children of God bringing joy and pleasure to our Father's heart.

On a practical level, our unity comes from participating in the bigger story of which we've all been called to be a part. Voltron came together because the individuals saw the need and joined forces to beat the enemy and save the planet or galaxy. In the same way, keeping the story of God before us, his mission and purpose, shows us the need to work together and set aside the things that don't matter for the sake of others.

Exploration

As a missionary, I made several trips to countries and met many Christians from other cultures. When I was in India, one man in the church there shone with the light of God's love. It emanated from him. He looked and dressed differently than me, lived in a very different culture, but he was my brother. I had to get to know him. The struggle to get beyond language and cultural differences was totally worth it. I discovered the treasure of Christ in another.

Many Christians have the same experience in missions, but it is also easy to live in our own cultural bubbles, even in church, basing our choices on what makes us culturally or politically comfortable. How do you engage people, believers and nonbelievers, that look and live differently than you? How do you choose to be uncomfortable to love brothers and sisters that differ from you?

Take stock and brainstorm opportunities you might have to engage and love.

Father, we praise you that your Church is so beautiful, full of people of different languages and colors and gifts and expressions. Help us see opportunities to get out of our comfortable cultural bubble and engage with and learn from believers of different denominations, traditions, political views, cultures, and languages, all to discover the beautiful unity and diversity within Christ. Amen.

Chapter 7
Dignity, Relief, and Empowerment

Being a part of the missionary community in Korea, my wife and I were involved in many conversations on the nature of missions and the changes that should happen as we move forward. We read books and discussed these principles with fellow missionaries in several contexts. The world of missions and denominations has continued to evolve, often in necessary ways to better reflect the Gospel, Scripture, and the heart of God toward people.

After moving back to America, we were fortunate to get involved with our current church network, the Phoenix Community of Atlanta. Much of their practice and vision aligned with our background and experience, and the church's approach to missions was a huge part of our attraction to the group.

When Phoenix goes on a mission trip, we operate under the authority of the locals, a pastor or leader in that community. Local leaders understand best what the community needs and how to minister based on cultural perspectives and communication. We don't give anything to people on the trip. We do not hand out candy or give gifts to kids. Rather, we check with the pastor and supply him with the resources, and he facilitates giving.

Also, we go back to the same areas because the most important part is the relationship between us and the people in the village or community. We must see each other as people. Relationships are more eternal than physical resources, and those friendships are our primary goal.

Phoenix also believes in the skills and talents of the local population. The community has skills to be used for sustainable growth and transformation. Once we agree on a project under the local leadership, we hire people in the village or surrounding community to work, even if we are working, as well.

More and more mission organizations and churches are operating under similar principles. As we engage the world to show compassion, we must remember the wholistic approach combining three principles: dignity, relief, and empowerment.

Dignity

It is natural to think if someone needs our help, we must have or know more than they do.

This is a lie.

On one level, looking at a bank account or how big our houses are, we may have more physical resources. However, those aren't what matter in life, and if we translate it into a feeling of superiority, then we do more damage than good. Even if we give everything to the poor, if we don't do it in love, it's a waste (1 Corinthians 13). Our *charity* does no good if we end up devaluing the people we are there to help.

Our charity does no good if we end up devaluing the people we are there to help.

The value of a person is intrinsic, on a core spiritual level. God is the standard by which we measure. To him, our abilities or wealth aren't what give us value. My ability to speak or not, hear or not, see or not, walk run or not, my youth or age do not matter. My intelligence or lack thereof, my career choice or the number of credit cards I pay off, none of it makes God love or value me any less.

Each human being is created in the image of God (Genesis 1:36), that spark of the eternal within us distinguishing us from all creation (Ecclesiastes 3:11). We were fashioned by his hands, fearfully and wonderfully made (Psalm 139:14). When he created us, he prepared an awesome story for each one to live out if we would simply follow him (Ephesians 2:10). God thought about us before our conception, and his only thought was good and love.

CS Lewis said, "There are no ordinary people. You have never talked to a mere mortal." Every individual has eternal worth to God, completely separate from what we can do. God doesn't need what we can do for him. He wants our hearts, that eternal part he created, reconciled back to him. He can do the rest through us.

As desperate, destitute, or degenerate as a person might be, they have worth to God. Also, no amount of worldly accomplishment or accumulation gives anyone more value.

Every person has the potential to be a world changer with God. The most important part of that statement is *with God*. Rich, poor, old, young, master athletes or people dealing with severe disabilities, it doesn't matter.

The Gospels make a point to show us how Jesus dignified and reached out to people the Jews would have considered unclean—an oppressive tax collector like Zacchaeus; the ten lepers; the criminal on the cross; the woman with an issue of blood. The woman at the well was a Samaritan half-breed, a religious heretic, and a woman with many husbands. And yet he met her at the well, reached across cultural and religious lines, and gave her one of the clearest declarations of himself as the Messiah in the book of John.

We must never see people as less or unworthy or even unlikely. The Jubilee didn't make that distinction. Neither does God, and neither should we. Relationship is required—asking questions, looking people in the eye, inquiring about their stories, finding out what people do well, affirming them as human beings and listening. This is dignity.

All charity fails if we fail in this.

Relief

There are situations where the need is so dire and urgent, all we can do is give relief. If someone is starving, the first act is to feed them. If someone is naked, we must clothe them. For those dying, we administer care. In the story of the Good Samaritan, we find a man left for dead, totally unable to help himself, so the Samaritan provided.

Lazarus was dead and required someone else, Jesus, to give him life.

The act of direct relief reveals the salvation of God. We just give—not because people are worthy or unworthy, but because there is genuine need. God gave this example. He first loved us when we were dead in our sins. He reached out to us when we were unable to even know him in any real way.

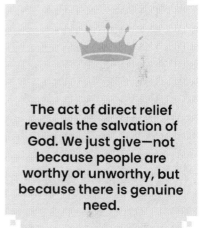

The act of direct relief reveals the salvation of God. We just give—not because people are worthy or unworthy, but because there is genuine need.

Giving to the poor was such a common occurrence in the ministry of Jesus, he commands it to the crowd in Luke 12:33. When Judas left to betray the Son of God, in the middle of the night, during a major holiday, the disciples assumed he was going out to give to the poor (John 13:30).

We should always seek for opportunities to give to those in need, but doing so in dignity and love requires more than simple relief. We must empower others as well.

Empowerment

God didn't just forgive my sin debt and save me from death and hell. He did that, yes, but he did more, which is the whole point of this book.

He filled me with his own Spirit. He gave me the power to live a life of peace and hope and love. God placed his very presence within us, sharing his divine power and authority with his children by heavenly birth.

When most people think about charity or giving to the poor, they conceive of direct relief. However, we aren't preaching the Gospel through our charity if that's where we stop. We must also empower people to live the story God has for them, whatever it looks like.

Jesus's ministry was full of moments where he empowered people, notably when opening the eyes of the blind and causing the lame to walk (Matthew 9:27-29). Christ also gave commands and purpose in conversations with people, especially to go out and preach the Kingdom of God (Luke 9:60). How much would a life change to go from blindness to sight? Being able to walk again? Those are only symbols of the transformational reality of the Kingdom.

There are great programs and parachurch organizations, like the aforementioned Atlanta Mission. Empowerment requires more than a program, though. It requires relationship, knowing someone, listening and seeing the unique talents and potential in each person. Empowerment also goes beyond individual relationship.

It takes a community to roll away the stone between people and Christ, by his direction. One of the common threads we see when dealing with the poor and those in need is the lack of what we call *relational resources*. In other words, when trauma or hardship occur, some people have family or friends that can help them get by as a safety net of sorts until there are opportunities to recover.

For example, I lost my job in 2009 amidst the Great Recession, and even though I took on part-time work, we still needed to live with my parents for a time. The situation worked because my parents have a decent sized house and the means to help.

Many don't have relational resources, so when hard times occur, they fall farther into crisis since they don't possess the relational network to cushion the fall and help them recover more quickly..

Part of the redemption is made available in a new family—the church. Within the dynamic of a local congregation, people in crisis find those connections because the Church is modeled after the family. Within the family of God, people in need can find work, opportunity, a second chance, education, training, encouragement, and love.

Exploration

During our time in India, our friend and apostle Pastor Daniel brought us to one of his Mercy Homes, a type of orphanage where orphans (ten or less) were placed in a home with parents, often church planters. They lived in a home, in a neighborhood, and went to school.

The seven girls in the home we visited lined up and told us their goals. "I want to be a teacher." "I want to be a preacher." "I want to be a doctor." One girl had bright eyes and was alive in the Spirit of God.

Pastor Daniel leaned over to me and whispered, "You see that girl?" He pointed at the girl with bright eyes.

"Yes," I said.

"I bought that girl from prostitution for fifty dollars," Pastor Daniel said.

Now she was in a home with sisters and parents, and she dreamed of becoming a teacher. Dignity, relief, empowerment.

I started crying because it was so beautiful. I couldn't help it. I'm crying now as I write it.

She's only one example, along with the Mercy Homes in India, of how creative and impactful we can be with God when we are generous as Christ with others.

Father, thank you for how you saw us, loved us, saved us from hell, and then empowered us by your Spirit to live and walk in intimacy and purpose with you. Help us to never look at those with less as if they are less. Give us your eyes to see the potential and value in each person no matter their worldly situation. Amen.

Chapter 8
Supernatural Expression

In Steven Spielberg's classic, *ET*, Elliott introduces the alien to his older brother and younger sister. The creature is weird and different, and questions abound. What is this being? ET begins to express his desire to *go home*. But where is home?

ET proves he comes from another world by doing miraculous, seemingly impossible actions. He levitates clay in an active model of the solar system, and his chest lights up. Elliott and his siblings help him build a gizmo to *phone home*. During that sequence, Elliott nicks his finger, and there's a little blood.

The alien heals the cut with a finger that lights up.

On the way to the woods to set up the communicator gizmo, ET and Elliott fly over the trees on the boy's bike, setting up one of the most iconic visuals in movie history, their silhouette across a full moon.

The Scripture calls us aliens and strangers in this world (2 Peter 2:11), reborn from heaven. Jesus was the pioneer and initiator of that incarnation, and one way he manifested the Kingdom was through miraculous displays of God's power, healings, resurrections, etc. As Christians, *little Christs*, we have the same calling and ability.

Jesus gives a few versions of the Great Commission, and in Mark 16, after the instruction to preach the Gospel, Christ says miraculous signs will follow those who believe. He then lists a few, like speaking in other languages, casting out demons, and healing the sick.

In context, Jesus promises we will do miracles while on his mission. This doesn't exclude miracles in other situations, necessarily, but Jesus didn't say, "Go ahead and live your life and supernatural signs will follow you." The design is that supernatural acts will happen through walking with God and his purpose, the Good News.

I have seen miracles throughout my whole life following Christ, but I can honestly say my wife and I saw far more during our time as missionaries in Korea. A change of geography isn't the secret. However, we were more on mission for God than ever before, giving up our American life and careers for something greater and more eternal, all in obedience to God through relationship. And we saw the fruit of obedience in many ways, one of which was more healings and miracles.

As an important caveat, the Bible never promises God will heal every sick person or that his power will fix every physical or worldly problem. Tragic events will happen in this life, and we will grieve and weep for them as we should.

These miraculous events are declarations of another reality, one we can enter and live within through the death and resurrection of Christ and our full commitment (Luke 10:9). As aliens in this world, living in the power of God on his mission, we can't deny that miraculous signs are part of the Jesus Model in sharing the Good News. Again, Lazarus rose from the dead as a symbol that Jesus himself is the resurrection, speaking of something more eternal and lasting.

But we must start where Jesus did. And that's in prayer.

Prayer

To be honest, we could have discussed prayer at any point in this book. Prayer undergirds every part of our walk.

I include it here to remind us that before Jesus said, "Lazarus, come forth!", he prayed to his Father. God the Son *lifted his eyes* and addressed God the Father. Jesus even admits the prayer itself was a sign so people would believe. Believe in what? Believe God sent him. Believe what was about to happen was dictated from heaven.

Make no mistake, prayer is miraculous. Through Christ, we have unfettered access to the very throne room of God (Hebrews 4:16), able to make our requests before him as children to a Father who loves us immeasurably more than we can understand (Philippians 4:6-8). God's activity and purpose is to reconcile all creation back to himself through the Son, the Lord Jesus Christ. When we use prayer to make requests along his purpose (in the name of Jesus), then miraculous things are bound to happen.

Make no mistake, prayer is miraculous.

I don't think we understand the power of prayer. God began to really teach me more about prayer while in Korea—while more on mission, which wasn't a coincidence. He told me, "If you knew how powerful I am, all you would do is pray." Years later, I'm still learning.

Prayer is the ultimate act of faith, as all miracles result from faith. Jesus separated himself to pray alone with the Father, *as was his custom.* (Luke 22:39) He also prays here in the Lazarus narrative. If he needed to pray, we need it far more.

In his teaching to the disciples on prayer, the Lord's Prayer includes a request of the Kingdom coming to earth, for God's loving from heaven to be done here (Matthew 6:9-13). We address him as Father. The prayer has a collective point of view, using plural personal pronouns. "Our Father …" We pray with the community in mind. After requesting his Kingdom to come, we pray for our provision in that context, like Matthew 6 where we are to "seek the Kingdom of God above all else, and live righteously, and he will give you everything you need."

Prayer also acknowledges there are spiritual, unseen roots of the problems of brokenness and corruption we are addressing. There is an enemy out to kill, steal, and destroy. To only minister to what we see without fighting against the enemy behind it all will be fruitless.

For us to roll away the stone, and remove the barriers between the dead and Christ, prayer must be where we start. This is God's work and must be done with his direction and power.

Healing and Miracles

A friend of mine came to me one night while we were hanging out in Korea. He said, "I gotta tell you something, Britt. I've been on bipolar medication for years. You spoke the other night about forgiving your father, and I realized I needed to forgive mine. In worship, I forgave my dad, and I felt something come off me. A great weight lifted. God told me I didn't have to take the medication anymore. So I stopped. It's been a couple of weeks and I've been fine. God totally healed me."

He's been healed ever since.

This is but one example of my personal experience regarding the miraculous. I've seen money show up in my bank account. We've seen food multiply. We've laid hands on people and seen them immediately healed. We've prayed for a student a hundred miles away after a serious injury, possibly unto death, and the doctors reported his quick recovery as a miracle.

And more.

I'm not telling people to stop taking medication for some sort of illness, nor am I saying that every injury, sickness, or problem will be supernaturally fixed. God doesn't always respond with a miracle, and he's still good even when he doesn't. A temporary situation doesn't change an eternal reality. It also takes the supernatural power of God to show grace and hope during tragedy and trauma. Even death can't usurp God's goodness, power, and redemption.

However, there will be miracles when we walk with God in his purpose. Sickness, disease, injury, death, these result from the fall and the work of the Devil. Jesus came to undo them, and there will be moments when God breaks forth to show off and give physical manifestation that the supernatural is real.

Healings and miracles don't have a formula. Jesus didn't read a book or take a seminar to learn how to heal people with blindness by spitting in the dirt, making mud, and rubbing it on their eyes (John 9:1-12). The root remains the same—walk in an obedient relationship with God. As Christ explained to Nicodemus, the people born of the Spirit are like the wind (John 3:8). You can't figure them out, there won't be a formula. The formula is to follow the Spirit.

Gifts of the Spirit

Another expression of the supernatural is the gifts of the Spirit.

These aren't talents or abilities we naturally possess, even though those are unique and individual and can be used by God. Gifts of the Spirit are supernatural abilities given to us when we are reborn for two main purposes—encourage the body of Christ (1 Corinthians 12:4-23) and be a witness to the world.

The latter is pertinent to this part of our discussion, our engagement with people outside the church. As part of the Great Commission in the Gospel of Luke, Jesus told them to go but to first wait for the power of the Spirit, the anointing that would make them witnesses of the death and resurrection of Christ.

Witnesses to who? The world. How can we be witnesses of the resurrection in our own power? We can't. So they obeyed, waited, and God sent the Spirit, and then they spoke in different languages to declare the awesome works of God. (Acts 2)

They didn't just get the Spirit to be nicer people, although a change in nature and character is part of it. They started doing miraculous things.

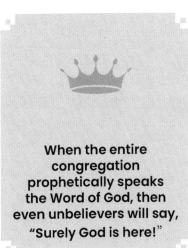

When the entire congregation prophetically speaks the Word of God, then even unbelievers will say, "Surely God is here!"

Another central passage is where Paul discusses the order of their worship gatherings in 1 Corinthians 14. He explains that speaking in tongues should have an interpreter, for the sake of unbelievers, and that when the entire congregation prophetically speaks the Word of God, then even unbelievers will say, "Surely God is here!"

In line with that theme, Paul teaches we should desire spiritual gifts, especially that we may prophesy (1 Corinthians 14:1). New Testament prophecy isn't telling people the future, although it can include that. The principle of prophecy in the NT is telling other people what God told us to say. We listen to God and speak his words. Peter says, "when you speak, speak the oracles of God." (1 Peter 4:11).

That's how Jesus lived. He only did what he saw the Father do and only said what he heard the Father say. We can get weird and denominational about the term *prophecy*, but it's that simple. It's the Jesus Model we continue to use.

The enemy loves for us to get into arguments with the world about what is right and wrong or who to vote for or what political party is the greater evil. But that's a distraction from the mission and not the best we can give others (2 Timothy 2:23). The revelation of God is the most precious thing in existence, and if we love others, we will tell them what God is saying to them from heaven. Speak the oracles, the prophecies, of God to them.

Even though it might be a short or simple statement, a prophetic word to them will have more impact than any apologetics, emotional appeal, or intellectual wrangling. God knows what people need to hear more than we do, and he wants to show them love more than we do. Trust him. Listen and speak. We don't have to prove we are right. We must love, and the best way to love is with the message of God.

Every spiritual gift is dependent upon the gift of hearing and doing what God says. They're his gifts to us. He knows best how to use them. Let him teach us how to leverage the word and power of heaven to engage the world and reveal Christ.

Exploration

One way we can see more miracles is to tell stories. Develop a discipline of sharing stories of God's miraculous power with each other and with nonbelievers.

People need hope to survive, and in a world of brokenness and tragedy, hope is hard to find. When the impossible happens, a miracle reveals there's more to life than we've imagined. We long for the impossible, and with God, all things are possible. Miracles move us closer to the reality that the supernatural is real. They give us hope that something better is possible.

In the Old Testament, after the Lord stopped the waters of the Jordan River and the people crossed, God commanded Israel to set up Ebeneezers, stones that would initiate telling the story of God's work

(Joshua 4:4-7). The apostles and others wrote down the stories of Jesus in the Gospels and Jesus followers in Acts. These stories were markers to help remember.

What are yours? Find ways to remind yourself of those times God did a supernatural work in your life. And then tell others.

Father, thank you for your supernatural interventions in our life, beginning with salvation and being reborn by the Spirit, and continuing with the miracles we see through our walk as we follow you. Help us tell the stories of miracles to spur us all on to more in Christ. Amen.

Chapter 9
Walk in Righteousness

My first favorite sport was soccer, but when we moved from the city of Montgomery to outside of Atlanta, soccer wasn't a thing. Being tall and thin, I switched to basketball. This made my father happy since he was an All-State high school player in West Virginia. He was ready to teach me a thing or two.

First, he gave me Bill Sharman's ancient, black and white book, *Sharman on Basketball Shooting*. I learned little from the book. But when Dad took me out to a basketball hoop and showed me, I began to lay the foundations of what it meant to be a good, if not great, shooter. The footwork, the placement, the focus, all of it. The result? I became a good shooter with an amzing example to emulate.

We can't earn our salvation through our own effort, and the Scripture makes it clear our righteousness is only *filthy rags*. However, that doesn't mean it doesn't matter what we do, especially given the power of the Holy Spirit.

Yet, it is a common conversation within the Christian community. "I can't help but sin. All God sees is Jesus, not me."

The same power that forgave all the sins of the world also rescued us from hell, beat death, created the universe, ordered life from the smallest minutiae to galaxies, put to death all enmity that exists and more. That power can't help us live according to Christ? Of course it can.

The standard of righteousness is clear in the New Testament. Paul says the believers should "imitate me as I imitate Christ" (1 Corinthians 11:1), and he and those with him lived *blameless* while among the Thessalonians (2:10-11). The apostle John writes, "Dear children, don't let anyone deceive you about this: When people do what is right, it shows that they are righteous, even as Christ is righteous." (1 John 3:7) Paul requests prayer for his life, for his actions to line up with the Gospel so that he's not found to be a *counterfeit* (1 Corinthians 9:27). The Gospel he preached to Agrippa (Acts 26) was to repent and do the works consistent with repentance. The New Testament isn't hiding this.

It matters what we do. At the same time, it matters what power we use when we act.

What does this mean? God cares what we do, how we live, and treat people. His commands are for our good and the good of others. As a God of love, he doesn't want us to hurt ourselves and others.

It matters what we do. At the same time, it matters what power we use when we act. Our own? That's our righteousness and means nothing. God's power? That's the secret. Now we're on the right path.

Our transformation isn't according to the right program, doctrine, or moral law. We are transformed by the renewing of our mind (Romans 12:2-3), thinking according to heaven. Then we live and walk in the righteousness of Christ.

The Righteousness of Christ

I need to deal with the statement "When God looks at me, he doesn't see me, he only sees Jesus." Of course he sees me. He sees me intimately, knows my every thought, knows the hairs on my head, and knows things about me I can't even know about myself (Luke 12:7). He doesn't give me the righteousness of Christ because he can't stand to look at me. He loves me. He knows and calls me by name, as he did Lazarus at the tomb.

God gives me the righteousness of Christ so I can walk, rest, and trust in him, not my own power and moral understanding. By dying to myself, my own will, and submitting myself to the Father, the righteousness of Christ is free to flow through me. Then it is no longer I who live but the eternal Christ who lives through me (Galatians 2:20-21). I live by a righteousness I can't take credit for nor claim as my own. But I am living according to the right standard.

We've been translated into a heavenly realm where the rules are different. Our thinking must change according to those rules, from manufacturing a righteousness by our own understanding and power to complete reliance upon the Christ that has been born within us. That Spirit has never sinned and never will.

Temptation isn't a sin. Jesus was tempted in every way, even with things we can't imagine. It wasn't easy for him, either. Struggling with a will contrary to the Father also isn't sin. Jesus struggled in the Garden of Gethsemane (Matthew 26:36-46). Yet he submitted to the Father and obeyed. He overcame by seeing the goodness of God and the hope beyond the moment. Sin, therefore, is giving in to temptation, not the temptation or the struggle itself.

The Devil gets involved here, too. Our own desires tempt us, yes, but he also places thoughts in our head, evil and crazy thoughts. Have you ever had a crazy thought from nowhere? It didn't come from nowhere. The Devil whispers the crazy thought in one ear and then speaks in the other ear, "How can you think like that and call yourself a Christian? You're not!" But he put the thought there in the first place.

Our thoughts are important, but they are not our identity. We can take those thoughts captive and replace them with truth (2 Corinthians 10:3-5). My mentor used to say, "You can't help if a bird lands on your head, but you can stop it from building a nest there."

What we do when we're alone is who we really are. Righteousness, or spiritual self-control, works from the inside out. It's not about a performance but the way we live, and that begins when no one is looking. We're not trying to impress anyone. In fact, we're told to confess faults to each other (James 5:16). Our first responsibility of leadership is our own heart and mind. When we learn those lessons, God will give us leadership in other areas.

When we sin or miss the mark, we plead the blood of Jesus and return and try again. We return to walking not by our human nature but by the Spirit.

Walking by the Spirit

Another famous scripture explains this. "There is therefore now no condemnation to those who are in Christ Jesus, who do not walk according to the flesh, but according to the Spirit." (Romans 8:1-2; NKJV)

Who has no condemnation? Those in Christ Jesus. Where should I make sure I am? In him, in Christ. How do I do that? Who are in Christ? Those who don't walk according to the flesh but according to the Spirit. What should my focus be? Reject the reliance upon my human nature, my strength and ability, and trust only in the revelation and power of the Spirit of God.

The Spirit isn't a mystical force or a general attitude. He's a person. To walk according to the Spirit means I seek his counsel in my everyday decisions and then rely upon his power. That is being *in Christ* and having *no condemnation*.

My own human nature is the problem and can't be the solution. What happens when I use my human nature to try to manage my human nature? I just strengthen the human nature, the problem (Colossians 2:23), and that's the self-destructive evil of legalism. My nature is dead and can only produce death. But I can't even consider my human nature dead; I can only put to death the deeds of the flesh by the Spirit.

I must constantly remind myself of these simple and profound ideas, brainwash my mind to renew it according to what is eternally true, then my actions will reflect the life of God.

Evidence of a Changed Life

Circumstances are true in the unseen before they manifest in what is seen.

This is a principle of the Kingdom we would do well to remember. We are given the Spirit and the righteousness of Christ, then they flow through us in ways people can see. We live and act differently.

Brian Holland of Phoenix Community of Atlanta often says, "The evidence of a changed life is a changed life." I can tell people all I want how Jesus changed me, but it must be evident in how I live. The apostle Paul has a great conversion story, getting knocked off his horse and blinded on the road to Damascus (Acts 9). However, Paul's almost scandalous teachings on grace never included a statement, "Well, I still kill Christians and put them in jail. I just can't help it. Thank God I'm forgiven!"

God doesn't give us his power without his character. We need both in tandem. God's power without his character makes us abusive. The gifts of the Spirit require the fruit of the Spirit (Galatians 5:22-23). God produces both. God within us produces godly character—love, joy, peace, patience, kindness, generosity, faithfulness, gentleness, self-control. The language of *fruit* is about something organic, not manufactured.

> **God doesn't give us his power without his character. We need both in tandem.**

Fruit is evidence of the root. If you tell me you have an apple tree, then it should produce apples, not oranges. "You can identify them by their fruit, that is, by the way they act." (Matthew 7:16) Our character and actions are evidence of something. Let them be of Christ.

Fruit gives sustenance to others. Our character brings hope and peace to others, at least temporarily, giving a taste of the eternal love of God. The fruit of the character of God appears in every situation and circumstance, in every season of life.

Fruit is also a means of multiplication. Within the apple, at its core, is the seed for another entire apple tree. The character of God through us is part of preaching the Gospel.

This isn't about uniformity, as if the change in me must look exactly like yours or the other way around. Yes, there are moral standards in the Bible. Yet, we may see a Christian who isn't very nice and question their faith, but we don't know from what situations or life circumstances God saved them. The point is transformation and growth in a Christ-centered life.

Because it must be repeated, our goal isn't to produce a complete, moral life. That is something we can't do. Christ has already done it. Our goal is to walk in tune with the Spirit, and the natural result will be a righteous life.

When shooting a basketball, my goal is to hit the shot, but my focus is on my foot placement, how I use my knees, the form of my arms, what my eyes concentrate on, and the follow through. When those fundamentals are right, I will hit the shot more than I miss. The fundamentals are the discipline. When you do them over and over, they become a part of you, automatic. That is renewing your mind.

Living a righteous life is impossible. That is why Jesus had to accomplish it for us and place his Spirit within us to live through us. With God, all things are possible (Matthew 19:26). Peter did the impossible, walking on water, while his eyes were focused on Jesus. His failure to do the impossible came when his eyes lost that focus (Matthew 14:22-31).

John wrote letters with the purpose of encouraging us not to sin (1 John 2:2). But if we sin, he said, it's not hopeless. We haven't lost it all by getting off track. We have an advocate with the Father who forgives all. Turn back and cling to him.

Exploration

I have sinned. Seriously messed up. I knew what was wrong, and I did it even as a Christian.

Because I have the Spirit in me and a conscience, I feel guilty when I sin. The Spirit is grieved. The Devil takes the guilt and manipulates it, telling me I'm not a Christian or a host of other things to get me to give up. To quit.

I end up going to the Father, thinking, "He will be really mad at me. I deserve some serious punishment." God's response is different. He agrees that what I did was wrong, but when I repent and turn to him in truth, his attitude is, "Good. You're back. Now let's get moving forward again." Moving forward might include me asking forgiveness, from him or others. God isn't out to punish me. That's not his goal. Now that I've restored the intimacy with him, he sets me back on purpose.

We can't be bad enough or sin enough for him to not want us with him. There may be some consequences in this life, but God will redeem all things if we return to a loving, committed relationship with him.

Father, thank you for your forgiveness and love to remove our sin and its penalty. Thank you for the power you've given us to walk worthy of the call in Christ Jesus. The power is yours and we choose to rest in you and follow you in all things. Amen.

Chapter 10
The Story of the Gospel

There are several moments in movies that will make me cry. At the end of the *Fellowship of the Ring*, when Sam won't let Frodo go without him. Also during the finale of *Return of the King* when Frodo says goodbye. See a theme? There are more.

While a teen, I went to the theater to see *The Karate Kid*, and I immediately wanted to sign up for martial arts. I wasn't the only one. New karate studios opened all around us.

Stories matter. Stories have an impact.

So far, rolling away the stone has been mostly based on our activity, how we treat people and engage the broken and hurting in our communities that need hope. The testimony of how we live is part of sharing the Gospel.

But we should never dismiss the importance of actually using words. What we say to people matters. Faith comes by hearing the word of God by a sent people. To heal the sick, give food to the starving, and fight against injustice alone is insufficient. Remaining silent is a refusal to participate in sharing the Good News, an incomplete Gospel at best.

The first mark of the anointing of the Holy Spirit was a supernatural speaking in languages about the wonderful works of God, the natural outgrowth of tongues of fire (Acts 2).

One of the primary fears for people is speaking in public. Because of our focus on fundamentalism and the neotraditional idea of an educated, charismatic speaker evangelizing, we shy away from sharing the Good News with others. We can mix in there the worldly resistance to listen, the *keep your religion to yourself* vibe, and a general feeling of religious obligation in the church when it comes to *evangelism*. Either way, people share the Good News less and less.

However, the Bible never makes sharing the Good News dependent upon a Master of Divinity degree, a title, or a specific event. Doctrine and theology are important and should be part of teaching, but we must focus on sharing eternal truth with those that are broken and in need of hope, how to remove the barriers between the dead and the life-giver Jesus.

Jesus is our model. In part of his confession to Pilate, Jesus said he came to testify and be a witness to the truth (John 18:37). Him, as a person. He came to live among us. He lived a story within a human life. The eternal Son of God submitted himself to a temporary, chronological story. He started in the womb, was born in Bethlehem, raised in Nazareth, and so on.

He also told stories. We call them parables. He never taught without telling stories (Mark 4:34). Neither should we.

The Power of Story

Jesus didn't *only* tell stories, but stories are the secret. Theology and doctrine are important, and we should regard them seriously, and yet, human language can't properly contain eternal truth. We're expressing something eternal in a limited delivery system.

A story is complex and deep, less limited. Even a simple story possesses a certain amount of depth. A narrative can communicate eternal reality in a way that a theological definition can't.

Jesus never gave a definition for the Kingdom of God, nor did any writer of the New Testament. But Jesus would say, "The Kingdom of Heaven is like …" and then teach by telling a story.

Stories have important elements. First, stories are personal and relational. We tell stories when we get to know people. An argument divides. Stories invite others into more intimacy.

Second, stories place truth within relatable contexts. A woman lost a coin. A servant owes his master more than he can pay. Stories include us. Even a child, when reading or watching a movie, places him or herself in the place of the character.

Third, stories transcend and include both intellect and emotion, focusing on experience. Stories show that truth must be lived to be true. Truth matters and has an impact.

Fourth, stories reveal other possibilities. The impossible can happen. The darkest moments can be overcome. The woman finds the coin. The servant is forgiven great debt. Overcoming the impossible gives us hope, inspires us, and reveals a hint of another world. Our own stories can matter.

Stories tell us we're part of a bigger story.

Fifth, stories tell us we're part of a bigger story, for which we long to be a part. There's a bigger story going on beyond our day to day doing laundry, changing diapers, and cars breaking down. And that bigger story isn't just for the educated, charismatic, or especially talented but for everyone. Subsequently, that includes a call away from our current story to be a part of the bigger one. Our current story is too small.

Sixth, stories ask questions and activate curiosity. Stories lead us to dig further, to investigate. The disciples got frustrated with Jesus for telling stories. "Just tell us!" And he would go further into the meaning for those that wouldn't quit and endured through the confusion, those who want the treasure of truth enough to give their life for it.

Seventh, stories are simple. The Gospel isn't complicated, and often doctrinal discussions get complicated quickly. It is the temptation of the Devil to draw us away from the simplicity that is in Christ (2 Corinthians 11:13). Great stories keep it simple and supremely powerful.

Along the path of reaching out and living generously, we tell stories. Why? God is a storyteller.

The Story God is Telling

The Bible is a narrative. It literally says, "In the beginning …" and continues by explaining how sin entered the world through corruption and evil. Scripture reveals who God is by examining a very specific history of God's work and the reconciliation of all things to himself through Jesus. The four books we call Gospels are each a collection of stories with a beginning, middle, and end. Yes, Christ's teachings are all throughout, but it is in the context of a larger narrative.

The Bible doesn't tell us, but I can only imagine Lazarus told his story. A lot. He probably told it to everyone he ever met, within the first five minutes, and he wouldn't shut up about it. "So basically, I got sick and died, and then Jesus showed up and raised me from the dead!" The ultimate story-topper.

Let's keep it simple. Yin Kai disciples people to tell their God stories in three words. The first word should be what life was like before Jesus. The second word, what happened when you met Jesus, and the third word, what your life is like now.

Our story should reflect God's story, so we will begin with God's redemptive story in three words. First word, *corruption*. We live in a world bound in slavery to death and corruption. Second word, *Jesus*. The person of God in human form is the hinge of history. He's the difference-maker, the life-giver. The third word is *transformation*. All of creation is being transformed by the power of the Spirit and reconciled to the Father.

Now we can learn to tell our personal story.

Tell Our Story

Now that we are born again, our story is no longer our own. We have died, and now Christ lives his life in and through us. Just as Jesus was sent to be a witness and testimony to truth, Christ told them to wait for the anointing of the Holy Spirit to be witnesses unto God when they go to Jerusalem, Judea, Samaria, and the ends of the earth (Acts 1).

In Revelation, those that overcome do so by the blood of the Lamb, the word of their testimony, and not loving their own lives even unto death (Revelation 12:11). It's their own testimony, not repeating someone else's or guiding people to a pastor or leader. There's power in telling our own story transformed by Christ.

Every story will be unique, just as the different languages during Pentecost in Acts connected with different peoples, and that diversity is beautiful. There is even diversity in types of stories–parables were works of fiction, by the way. Yet the unifying factor is the transmission of the wonderful works of the God of love. Unity and diversity.

We are focusing here on stories from our own experience, however. An example is one of the most powerful moments in the popular series *The Chosen*, where Mary Magdalene is questioned about being delivered from a demon. Who did this? Her response: "Here's what I can tell you. I was one way and now I am completely different. The thing that happened in between was him."

This is the gift of every believer. For the reborn, we have the same story. It will include miracles, transformation, redemption, and deliverance in many forms and situations, but the truth revealed is the same. The life we live now reflects the eternal power and reality of Christ in us, our hope and peace. We tell others in love. "I was one way and now I am completely different. The thing that happened in between was him."

> **Every story will be unique ... yet the unifying factor is the transmission of the wonderful works of the God of love**

Our stories point back to him.

This doesn't mean we don't teach or make declarations of truth. Jesus did that too. He just never did it without a story.

With a life of generosity, righteousness, and justice, telling God's meta story and our personal God stories are keys that bring people into relationship. These stories inspire them and call them to the declarations of who God is and why he matters. Deeper conversations allow for eternal truth to be expressed in ways that have eternal impact.

Exploration

What is your story? Take time to go through the process of choosing three words. First word, what was your life like before Jesus? People often choose words like lost, confused, abused, wounded, forgotten, and abandoned. What is the second word describing what happened when you met Jesus? These could be words like freedom, love, peace, and healing. The third word is what your life is like now, terms like found, treasured, purpose, and empowered.

These are your three words, and they can change as you grow in God. The power is in the simplicity. Once you have three words, you can tell your God story in ten seconds, ten minutes, or an hour, depending on the situation.

My three words are *confused*, *commitment*, and *purpose*. I was raised in church but confused about what I was to do in life with all the different voices, denominations, and options that abounded around me. I was confused. Then God called me to commit fully to him and him alone. Commitment. After that, I was no longer confused. I had purpose. In every situation, I listened to him and obeyed the leading of the Spirit, giving me a simple focus and direction in all things.

Seek God in prayer, identify your three words, and share them with someone today.

Father, thank you for changing our stories, for living your life through us. Help us share our story and yours in a way that glorifies and praises you. Amen.

TWO

FLY

Life from the Dead

> *Jesus looked up to heaven and said, "Father, thank you for hearing me. You always hear me, but I said it out loud for the sake of all these people standing here, so that they will believe you sent me." Then Jesus shouted, "Lazarus, come out!" And the dead man came out* (John 11:41-44).

Jesus didn't ask for anyone's help with this part. No one could. Only God can do the impossible, raise the dead back to life.

We can't save anyone. All we can do is remove the barriers and introduce people to Jesus, and even that happens by his power. Yeshua (salvation) is the only name by which anyone can be saved. Once we introduce people to the Son, he does the work.

Christ begins with a prayer to the Father and then he calls the name of Lazarus. God knows us by name and loves us individually. He does this work within the hearts of individuals.

When the impossible has happened—we live again.

Growing up, I heard salvation explained like this: we're falling to our death, and with God's forgiveness, we've been given a parachute.

That might save us from death, but we're still falling. We're still bound by the power and law of gravity. That's not freedom.

The Scripture describes it in a different way. We haven't been given a parachute. We've been given wings. Now we can fly. That's freedom. That's being born again.

That's the second part of what Peter needs to learn to save his kids. He needs to *crow* and he also needs to *fly*, to live supernaturally. For us to join God in his work and purpose, we need a radical change. We need to live supernaturally and fly.

Chapter 11
The Work of God

My wife and I were married for four years when we found out we were pregnant. Convinced it was better for the baby and her, my wife wanted to proceed as naturally as possible. So we did what any educators would do. We read lots of books about how to do it all naturally.

We also had a community around us giving advice from their own experience. They told us their stories, which were extremely valuable. While we learned along the way, my wife would get frustrated when I refused to get worried about any of it, and she mocked my phrase, "It'll be all right. Women have been doing this for thousands of years."

I don't mean to dismiss problematic pregnancies in any way. They can be tragic. At the same time, the baby is on its way, and when done organically, my wife could walk for miles and eat eggplant parmesan until she puked, but the child would arrive when the time was right, probably a very inconvenient one. That's how life works.

It's funny to think of the immense amount of education we participated in just to do things *naturally*, but there's a reason those books exist. Our modern medicine has given us many advantages and progress, but it also makes us believe we can manufacture or contain something like childbirth. Believe me, if you've been around enough pregnant women, you know even people that try to control the process medically find there are always forces beyond their purview.

At some point, whether you're ready or not, your wife comes to you and says, "Um, the contractions are getting closer, and I think it's time."

What my wife and I had to learn about childbirth was to become a participant, flowing with the process as it naturally happened. It was and is beautiful.

It's the same in the spiritual. We can try to clean it up with programs and scheduling and worksheets, but we can't manufacture life from the dead. It is God's work. It will happen by his power on his timeframe, not ours.

Nothing happened until Jesus said, "Lazarus, come forth!" He waited days to arrive and could have waited longer once he stood before the stink of death. Either way, resurrection only happened when the one who is Resurrection and Life spoke the command.

This should place us at rest and peace. We can't save anyone. Never could. All we have to do is love others and live unto the Father.

Do what Jesus did. Pray to the only one who can do the impossible.

Access to the Throne

People sometimes mock prayer, whether in conversation or social media, as if an offer to pray for a person or situation is utterly useless.

Hopefully, by this point, you understand faith is active, not a lack of doing. To count prayer as useless only shows ignorance about the power of prayer.

And I can't judge that ignorance because I had it, too. For years, I would have parroted the notion that we should pray, even admitted a few of the older ladies of our church were *prayer warriors*, for those that remember the term. But because of my personality, being a male, or maybe an American, I didn't pray very often. I was more interested in feeding my intellect or staying busy with activity.

To learn about the power of prayer, we must have a proportional revelation about our own inability. I can do nothing—back to the filthy rags of my righteousness. The only thing that matters, what will last, is participating in the work of God.

My mentor used to say, "People say 'you're so heavenly minded, you're no earthly good.' But the opposite is true. Unless we're heavenly minded, we can't be any earthly good." This requires prayer.

Prayer is a work of God. One role of Jesus is as a mediator, standing before God on our behalf. Our lives are already in Christ, there at the right hand of God, and the purpose of prayer is to align us with what Jesus is already doing. Through being in Christ and the Spirit of the High Priest in us, we are also priests in the Kingdom.

Jesus prays before he calls Lazarus, recognizing that he is only revealing an eternal truth in the temporal.

Finished

Jesus declared while in the throes of death, "It is finished!" (John 19:30) How finished is *finished* when God says it?

Revelation 13:8 declares the Lamb, Christ, was slain before the foundation of the world. The death and resurrection of Jesus might have happened in our historical chronology two thousand years ago, but in reality, it was already an event in eternity, outside the limits of our time.

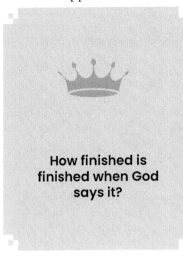

How finished is finished when God says it?

One gift of the Kingdom of God is that we are entering a perfect and complete realm already established and working, maintained by God. We can't grow or spread the Kingdom; it is infinite and eternal, unable to grow larger or smaller in any capacity. We can only enter (through the blood) and participate (through the indwelling Spirit) in what already exists. And we can invite others in, as well. We can participate in growing the population of those within the Kingdom, but not the heavenly realm.

We have no ability to achieve what matters or what lasts. The Old Covenant was between God and man and therefore failed since we couldn't fulfill our end. What was corrupted and human couldn't partner with the divine. The New Covenant isn't based on our ability at all, so that no person can boast (Ephesians 2:8-9). The New Covenant is between the Father and the Son, and we are a part of that covenant by being in Christ and Christ in us.

This is Good News. I walk with God by his power in what he has accomplished. I work from the rest of God. I give from the wealth of heaven. I fight from victory, not to attain it.

Jesus didn't ask for any help to call out Lazarus. No one could help and no one else should get the glory or credit. After rolling away the stone, the people just stepped aside.

Not Our Job

Jesus showed his model of leadership by taking off his clothes and washing the disciples' feet before the Passover, the act of the ultimate servant. Peter said, "you will never ever wash my feet," when it was his turn. (John 13:12-31)

Christ responded with a harsh statement. "Unless I wash you, you won't belong to me." We should note he would not force Peter to be served.

Peter changed his tune. He wanted to be part of Jesus. "Then wash my hands and head as well, Lord, not just my feet!"

We fight from victory, not to attain it.

But Jesus wouldn't do that, either. Why? Because God had already made the rest of Peter clean. Christ was only told to wash the *feet*, not clean the whole man. Jesus wouldn't step on what his Father had already accomplished.

We need to learn this, as well. There's a lot that just isn't our job.

The whole Christian life is all about God. It's all his job.

Before we knew he existed, he loved us first (1 John 4:19). He chose us (1 Peter 1:2-4), called us (2 Timothy 1:9), gave the gift of repentance and the grace to obey the Gospel (2 Timothy 2:25), gave us faith to see the unseen (1 Corinthians 12:9), gave us his divine nature through the new creation to walk with him (1 Peter 1:3-4), bestowed supernatural gifts (Ephesians 4:7-8), set up works in advance for us to do and prepares a place for us after death (John 14:3). He beat death. He is the resurrection. He is our peace (Ephesians 2:14) and righteousness, our hope.

There are hosts of other truths we could declare. It's all him.

Because he loves us, he gives us the power to choose. All we can do is take the gift of grace he offers and decide to trust and rely upon him, trading our life for his.

What a deal. No wonder heaven is full of constant, deafening worship. Knowing his work is complete, and we can rely upon his power and love, this is the root of thankfulness in our hearts. Hard times will come, but praise emerges from the Spirit within us to declare the finished work encompassed in what God has done, what he is doing, and what he will do.

The Gift of Repentance

Many don't like this term, *repentance*, for religious or other reasons. But the original sin wasn't simply the disobedience. That act was a result of a breaking of relationship. Adam and Eve seprated relationship from God. The Scripture doesn't say, "Eve was walking with God and came up to the forbidden tree." Doesn't say Adam was walking with God when he arrived, either. They both came to that place separate from constant relationship with the Creator.

It wasn't only Adam and Eve that left God. We have each left him, collectively and inividually, as a person and as people. Every one of us have gone astray in our hearts, dividing ourselves from he who is life, and the consequence for that is death.

But God doesn't want us to die, spiritually and eternally. With the core problem being relational, then the solution must be relational as well. God gives the opportunity through his Son for people to turn back to him, to submit our wills to his love and leadership, back to proper relationship in truth. We can't have right relationship based in a lie.

This is repentance. Willing reconciliation.

Repentance isn't something we can give or choose for other people. Repentance is a gift of God, like faith or anything else. We can't earn the ability to repent, nor can we give that ability to others. Repentance comes from God. Neither can we choose God for a person. Each of us must take that gift and participate in it, dying to self and living in Christ.

Salvation is God's work, and it is a miracle every time.

Exploration

Jim Elliot's quote is appropriate here. "He is no fool who gives what he cannot keep for that which he cannot lose."

And yet people are still foolish enough to reject God. Let's not pretend we can't understand why someone would do that. Haven't we rejected God? Whether in a moment or a season, haven't we each walked away from relationship with him? I know I have. Our salvation and endurance in faith shouldn't make us feel superior to anyone. We boast in God alone.

At the same time, we should weep for those that reject God. We love them and want what is best for them. It is right to desire the dead to live again. God does, so should we.

However, God forces no one, and we should take a cue from him. He loves, speaks, gives, and invites through Jesus, but he doesn't manipulate or coerce. Neither should we.

We love, invite, speak truth, and most of all pray for those we desire to see have a genuine change of heart. There is power in prayer.

Who are those people in your life? Who do you love and know that need to come back into loving and truthful relationship with Jesus? Pray for them and don't quit.

Father, thank you for accomplishing the work we couldn't do, for reconciling us back to yourself and one another through the Son, for beating death and sin and inviting us into that victorious life of the resurrection. Help us not to trust in our ways or understanding, but yours alone. It's all about you. No one else. Amen.

Chapter 12
Death to Life

Science has hypotheses, theories, and laws. One law of science is the Conservation of Mass. No new matter is ever created. It may change states or forms, but the same amount of matter exists before and after the change.

In fantasy stories, we can imagine something comes from nothing, calling it magic. But that is fiction. In our reality, everything comes from something. Unless we're dealing with a higher reality. Unless we're dealing with God.

God specializes in *something from nothing*. It's called creation.

The Father spoke this universe into existence through the Word, his Son, and he even set the design of how the world would operate. He ordered the laws of science in place and therefore transcends them.

Heaven operates by different rules and laws, a different culture, and a different form of matter (1 Corinthians 15). We needed a supreme solution to overcome the extreme problem.

Let's be clear about the problem. God didn't enter the world through Christ to make us feel better about ourselves, help us live a better American life or make minor improvements on our little kingdoms.

We were dead. Lifeless. Devoid of any ability to make any actual changes, if we even tried or cared. Utterly hopeless, that death and brokenness lead to an eternity of destruction and suffering. Hell.

CS Lewis describes it in *Mere Christianity* this way. We come to Christ thinking he'll enter into our nice cottage and fix the plumbing or give a new paint job, maybe replace the stove. Then God surprises us when he knocks down the whole structure and starts building something new. He's not out to fix our cottage. He's building a mansion for him to live in.

The Scripture calls the act of turning from death to life *repentance*, a choice of dying to self and living now to something new. The New Testament says we were dead, slaves.

This isn't hyperbole. In fact, the reality is much worse, and there is only one way out.

We build our lives on a lie that binds us to a law. Apart from God, we are slaves to that law.

The Law of Sin and Death

It turns out the fall in Genesis was a pretty big deal. First, our intimate relationship with God was severed, our very nature corrupted and twisted, and we were bound to death, struggle, and futility. We lost our purpose, our future, any meaning to our life.

Second, the whole of creation was subjected to that same futility and death. In science, it's called entropy. All things devolve into disorder and decay. A being or plant might be new and grow for a time, but eventually that living thing will grow old and die. No matter how much we fight it, that's the end of all things.

Romans 8 calls this the law of sin and death. I try to do right, Paul says, but I find I can't. That's the law of sin. The problem isn't simply that we do wrong, immoral acts. What Paul describes is an inner law, something within our very nature producing wrong behavior. The behavior is just the symptom of a deeper disease. Jesus taught it's not what comes into our mouths, what we eat, that makes us unclean. Our insides are already unclean, and unrighteous acts emerge from within (Matthew 15:11).

Unrighteous choices go against God's holy design and supreme law of life, and those have consequences. Death—the eternal, spiritual death and the physical one our bodies must endure.

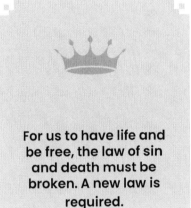

For us to have life and be free, the law of sin and death must be broken. A new law is required.

We can't get away from it. Everywhere we turn, we encounter a community, government or school ruled by the same corruption. Makes sense, right? They are built, run, and maintained by others bound by the law of sin and death. Even a supposedly perfect system is bound by the ones who maintain it.

Because of the choice Adam and Eve made, the whole world is now governed by the law of sin and death. Sin comes from death and returns to it. That's the cycle of slavery in which we live.

Paul says creation itself, the very matter of the universe, groans under the spiritual and physical oppression of entropy. Creation waits for the sons and daughters of God to be revealed for what they are and for the reborn to start living heaven on earth. Creation longs for it (Romans 8:22-23).

For us to have life and be free, the law of sin and death must be broken. A new law is required.

The Law of Spirit and Life

For God so loved the world that he sent his Son so we wouldn't perish but have eternal life. He broke the law of death that drags us down to hell with the shackles of sin, and he replaced the law with a better one that makes us free and brings us into the Kingdom of Heaven.

Through the death and resurrection of Jesus, of God in the flesh, we've been delivered from the kingdom of darkness and supernaturally rooted into the Kingdom of God. We were *translated*, per the KJV. Translated is a word similar to the transporter in *Star Trek*. We were in one place and then *poof!* Now we're somewhere else, a different realm, a Father's house.

My house, my rules, the old saying goes, and it's the same in the Father's kingdom. As I stated above, this realm operates by different rules. Sin and death can't enter that realm. Heaven operates by the law of spirit and life. Paul writes that the law of spirit and life breaks the law of sin and death.

The problem with the Old Testament law wasn't the ordinances. God passed down a covenant that, if followed, would lead to life. But if not, would kill them. The problem with the Covenant was simple—we had to keep it in our own strength (Romans 7:14). But we don't have the strength to live according to the divine. Death can't partner with life. That's why Paul says the Old Testament law is of death, because it depended on us to keep it.

Death must be destroyed and replaced with something of a different nature. Not the absence of law (not anarchy) but another, higher one.

My friend Dee explains it well. There is a law of gravity. It will hold you down. Fall from a high elevation and there will be a sudden stop. Splat. But another law can overcome the law of gravity. Planes and birds fly, overcoming gravity with the law of aerodynamics. Gravity no longer holds power over them. They are free by participating in a higher law.

The same is true in the New Covenant. Following the law of the spirit and life frees us from the law of sin and death, a reality only available to us through Christ.

God gave us wings, not parachutes.

> **The problem with the Covenant was simple—we had to keep it in our own strength (Romans 7:14).**

When contrasting sin and death with the spirit and life, we see the opposite of death is life. That makes sense. But I find it interesting the opposite of sin is the Spirit. Shouldn't it be righteousness? Paul chose his words carefully, inspired by the Holy Spirit. The opposite of sin is to follow God in a relationship through the Spirit, back to the design of Eden. Just replacing the old law with another moral standard doesn't break it, since it would still depend on us. We replace sin with a complete reliance upon the person who is righteousness. His acts, thoughts, and nature are all good, holy, and true. Following the Spirit will naturally result in a radically new life mirroring his acts, thoughts, and nature. Spirit and life is the new law we follow.

Living the New Life

Jesus was (and is) the model and pattern for the new life. He trusted in his Father, to the point where Christ admitted he didn't do his own will but submitted to the will of God. He only did what he saw the Father do and said what he heard the Father say. That's the pattern, clinging to the person of God who loves us and seeks our best in all things.

What did the life of Jesus look like? First, He lived godly character, making righteous choices and living holy. This is the fruit of the spirit. Second, the Lord also performed mighty miracles, healing the sick and raising the dead. These are the gifts of the Spirit. Third, he gave generously to the poor, feeding and encouraging those in need. Fourth, he taught with words and stories about the love of the Father and the Kingdom of God.

With Christ within us, that is our life, too.

We shouldn't misunderstand. The Scripture doesn't describe a dead human coming to life to continue as a human, and we aren't zombies.

To live heaven on earth we must be born from heaven, like Jesus.

We're no longer completely human. That's the key.

Exploration

The Scripture continually uses radical shifts to try to explain what has happened to us. Death to life (Ephesians 2:1-5). Darkness to light (Colossians 1:13). Slavery to freedom (Romans 6:20). Separate to an intimate member of a forever family. Despair to hope (Ephesians 2:12). Blindness to sight (2 Corinthians 4:4).

Nothing is more urgent than our spiritual state and what is happening in the unseen.

Yet we easily get distracted by what we physically see, situations in the immediate, forgetting for a time what is real in heaven. Therefore, we gather and remind each other of what is true, of our identity, and of the work of God upon which we must rely.

Along with our gatherings, we must develop disciplines to remind ourselves of these truths. These disciplines include prayer, scripture reading, singing praise, giving, serving, corporate worship, and others. The disciplines aren't the goal. They remind us of our living hope.

How do you remind yourself of the unseen realities, where your life really is in Christ at the right hand of God? How do you remind others? Reminders will anchor us in difficult times.

Father, thank you for transporting us from the kingdom of darkness into the Kingdom of your dear Son. We praise you for your love and mercy through Christ to give us all spiritual blessings. Help us surround ourselves with the church to remind us of truth and renew our minds with personal spiritual disciplines according to the revelation of heaven. Amen.

Chapter 13
New Creation

"It's alive!" Dr. Frankenstein screams in triumph once his grand experiment is successful. The doctor pieced together body parts from dead people and *created* something new and brought the being to life in his castle.

Mary Shelley's genius novel, however, isn't one of hope but horror. The creation is called a *monster*, and her book shows the terror of humanity. We are the true, abusive, and fearful monsters. The classic novel is a mirror to our fallen human nature.

The New Covenant isn't about making better people, nor is it about animating dead flesh. It's all about *new people*.

The New Covenant

I stood at a church function with a group of pastors and military chaplains around me, men I respected, men with Master of Divinity degrees and some with doctorates. I was on mission in Korea and God was teaching me more about the New Covenant. I asked these men, "What is the difference between the Old and the New Covenant?"

They couldn't nail down an answer or even a major difference. This bothered me. If there's not a difference, why did we need a new one?

To be fair, these leaders were at a social gathering and may not have felt prepared to answer a question like that from a weird dude like me.

But shouldn't we always be prepared to talk about the difference? The need for Christ? Jesus died and rose from the dead for this New Covenant. There must be a qualitative distinction.

The Old Testament clearly expresses the need for a New Covenant. The issue, once again, is the heart. Jeremiah 31 promises God will write his law on the heart and mind, the core from where all decisions flow. Included is the intimacy that all will know God, reconciled in a relationship with him. Ezekiel 36 promises God will remove the unresponsive heart of stone and replace it with a living one. He also designated a new spirit, placing his Spirit within us, and the Spirit will cause us to walk righteous, the law of Spirit and life.

The promised New Covenant, established by Christ at the Passover (Luke 22:20) would take care of the fundamental problem—the heart, our human and selfish nature unable to obey God. Our fallen human nature would be replaced by God's holy and complete nature that is now available in Christ. We're no longer completely human. We've been infused with the divine.

The Divine Nature

There are three ways to become part of a family. We can marry into one. We can be adopted. Or we can be born into a family. The New Testament uses all three to describe what has happened to us in Christ. That's a complete love. A sure thing.

Being married into the family is relational, intimate, becoming one with Christ by choice after being wooed and chosen by God (2 Corinthians 11:2). Adoption communicates how we were once not a part of the family but were picked from love (Ephesians 1:5). During the time the New Testament was written, an adopted child couldn't lose the family status and inheritance under Roman law; a natural born child could. Adoption also gives us security.

Marriage and adoption are amazing and loving gifts (included, chosen, and loved), but we can still be a created human and enjoy those. However, to have God's nature, and to be like Christ, we must be born from him. We are also begotten from the Father, and now have his Spirit within us, sharing the divine, eternal nature in Christ.

There is now a part of us that was never created. It is of the eternal, begotten from the Father like the Son. Jesus was the forerunner, the firstborn from the dead (Colossians 1:18). A new and second Adam (1 Corinthians 15:45).

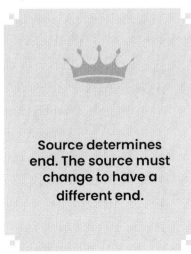

Source determines end. The source must change to have a different end.

Source determines end. The source must change to have a different end.

Adam was the source of all humanity, and the inevitable end of that Adam is death. To change the end from hell to heaven with the Father, God had to change the source. Adam, the nature of sin, and the power of death were ended and overcome on the cross by the Son. Adam, as a beginning, was replaced with the eternal Christ, which gives us his goal, eternal life with the Father. Jesus is the Alpha and Omega, the beginning and the end (Revelation 22:13).

Now we can be Christians, a word which means *little Christ*.

This is the new creation, born from heaven, both human and divine, and it is all that matters (Galatians 6:15). It changes everything. We must be born again.

The Immortal Spirit and Body

Translated now into the Kingdom and given the Spirit within us and the divine nature, we are immortal. Where is the sting or victory of death? Christ claims victory through the cross and resurrection.

Wait a minute, someone might say, Christians still die. The early believers asked the question, and Paul addressed it (1 Corinthians 15). We've been given a new spirit, an eternal one, and it is a seed and down payment for the new body we'll one day be given. The body we currently have is corruptible and cannot enter or survive heaven, since it is still made of temporary material. Therefore, Lazarus still died after his resurrection. Despite his longing, Moses couldn't see God's full glory while in his earthly body (Exodus 33:18-20).

That body, that flesh and blood body, can't inherit the Kingdom of God, Paul adds. Only the divine can.

We need a new body for heaven, one that is made of the same spiritual, eternal material as the rest of heaven, so we can commune with God face to face. Jesus had a different body when he was rose from the dead, like a superhero. He popped in and out of rooms and flew into the sky (John 20:19; Acts 1:9-12). His new body was made of heavenly substance and operated by heavenly rules.

God promises us a body like Jesus has. Since we have his Spirit, we'll be given an incorruptible, spiritual form. Not a ghost, though. The disciples could touch the resurrected Jesus, and John writes that Jesus ate food after he rose from the dead (Luke 24:42-43).

With a new nature, we have a new identity.

A New Name and Identity

God often changed people's names once they had an encounter with him. Coming into a relationship with God radically changes a person, to the point that a new name often becomes necessary. Abram became Abraham, the father of faith. Sarai became Sarah. Jacob became Israel. In the New Testament, we have Simon to Peter.

Names have meaning. When childless Abram was promised that he would birth a nation by faith, God changed his name to Abraham, which means father of many. God gives new names according to the new purpose and role we receive within our reconciled relationship to him.

> **Coming into a relationship with God radically changes a person, to the point that a new name often becomes necessary.**

There is no more radical change than what happens in the New Covenant, and Jesus mentions in Revelation how he gives individuals new names (2:17) that no one knows but the individual, an unseen identity.

We don't lose our individuality. God didn't change the identity of Abram, Sarai, Jacob, and Simon, to the same name as everyone else.

They were given a new identity, but still unique. Regarding the gifts, Paul says there is only one Spirit but many manifestations of the same gift. There isn't a different Holy Spirit in me than in you or anyone else. There is only one Spirit in all of us, but we are still unique new creations with separate purposes within the grand purpose. We are distinct stories reflecting God's universal redemptive story.

Our uniqueness follows us into eternity, into our new, resurrected body. Jesus showed up after death … with scars (John 20:20). Our story continues to be told, even the pain we endured and the tragedy and the agony God redeemed. Scars are stories, no longer open wounds, and they only emphasize the need to tell our stories. We'll be telling them in heaven.

A part of me believes eternity will be a continual sharing of God stories through our healed and redeemed scars.

For example, Revelation reveals the existence of a variety of nationalities and languages (Revelation 7:9), partly the result of the judgment of the Tower of Babel, now redeemed in praise and worship around the throne. God will redeem it all.

If we look at the cells of our blood through a microscope, it appears chaotic, like there's no organization. But once we step all the way back and perceive the whole body, there is the cohesive and unified full expression of a human. We see the same exact DNA in every individual cell doing its distinct work.

One day, with the full perspective of eternity, we will see such an expression of all the collective Church across thousands of years, and it will be a clear vision of Christ. In the meantime, we celebrate Christ in each of us and the whole, staying faithful with the part we've been given.

That's how we live free.

Exploration

The idea that the divine can coexist with humanity appears impossible. The Jews certainly thought so, despite the cryptic prophecies from the Old Testament. Later heresies, namely Gnosticism, resisted the idea of God in human, physical form, postulating Jesus was simply an apparition.

Scientists argued for decades whether light was a wave or a particle. There was evidence for both, but to be both was impossible. A wave couldn't be a particle nor a particle a wave. It had to be one or the other. But how to reconcile with the evidence? Scientists chose sides on the debate.

Eventually, the scientific community admitted what the evidence showed them. The impossible existed. Light is both a particle and a wave.

Through Christ, we are partakers in the impossible —the divine coexisting with the human in a loving relationship. The new creation.

Our identity is from Christ, but Christ in me will be unique from Christ in anyone else. Christ will still be evident, and that's the unity. God is so infinite and creative that he can express the same Christ in billions or trillions of different ways. It's beautiful.

This means we need your expression of the one God. It's not your truth, but your unique combination of gifts, talents, past, redemption, and purpose that no one else has or will have, all to express the one God. The church and the world need you to learn how to use those wings and fly free.

Father, thank you for making the impossible possible through Jesus and bringing us into eternal life with you. Help us to always remember we must rest and trust in you alone to participate in the impossible. Amen.

Chapter 14
Made Free

We use the word freedom often in the United States, likely more than in any other country or culture. We attach the term freedom to a great deal of things, and perhaps it's lost its meaning.

On a political level, we equate freedom with democracy, our republic, our right to vote, and similar ideas of the rights of individuals. Largely, our modern understanding of freedom centers on a simple, "Doing what I want to do." That has its issues, clearly. What if what I want to do stops someone else from doing what they want to do? What if what I want to do hurts others, kills them, or violates their rights? We soon find vastly different definitions of what those boundaries are and how to manage freedom in the sense of choice.

Don't misunderstand, the ability to make choices regarding our lives and property is one kind of freedom, or one element of it. We can make our own choices, but we are not free from the consequences of those choices. Even if a certain choice is legal, it doesn't make it right. Doing what is morally wrong has consequences for us and others. No matter what we believe or think, no matter what culture or government thinks, we will face those consequences.

The Bible makes this clear because there is a law above all others, the law of God, the standards of righteousness and holiness that he sets, not apart from him but emanating from him. He is holiness and righteousness and justice. That is the measure by which all things will be judged, from the individual to the government.

Benjamin Franklin made an insightful statement. "Only a virtuous people are capable of freedom. As nations become more corrupt and vicious, they have more need of masters." Freedom is not something given, necessarily, but something we are capable of, according to Franklin. If a people are virtuous, then they can be trusted with freedom. When a people become more corrupt and vicious, then they require more law, not less, a larger and more powerful government, not a smaller one. A corrupt people need tyranny.

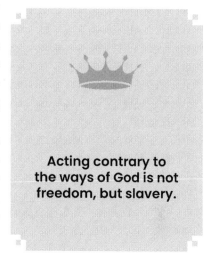

Acting contrary to the ways of God is not freedom, but slavery.

Acting contrary to the ways of God is not freedom, but slavery. Corrupt actions reveal we are bound to our own selfish desires, not some noble idea of living free. Choosing the opposite of God's design and nature is not only evidence of bondage but will lead us to more bondage. Sin leads to tyranny. Freedom, therefore, is the right to act and also choosing what is right. The latter is more important, necessary, and far more powerful.

One with the Truth

The crowd almost murdered Jesus after he told the newly believing Jews, "You are of your father, the Devil." (John 8) What? They were the people chosen by God, children of Abraham. Jesus explained they were "children of the Devil" because they acted like the Devil. They weren't children of Abraham, or they'd obey by faith, as he did. Their actions and choices revealed their true loyalty.

We have the right to choose, but those choices will come from a heart that's either free or enslaved. Outward law can only manage or punish that nature, not change it. We are slaves to whatever has power over us. We act and say, "Oh, I couldn't help it …" That's not freedom. In fact, to make excuses for what has power over us is to delve further into bondage.

Christ has set us free, which includes the ability to choose. The prison doors can be opened, but unless our hearts are changed, we will take bondage wherever we go. We are bound from our source, where we come from, the original Adam. Freedom, then, is more than being set free.

We must be free from within. We must be *made* free, created anew, reborn, free and unbound by our nature, our past, our thinking, and our previous source. God changed where we came from through Christ, and so our new nature, shared with the divine, is free of this world's boundaries.

Jesus uses this language at the very beginning of John 8. In the NKJV, he says, "You will know the Truth, and the Truth will *make* you free." The word there means both set and made free, not only one but both. Free from within.

Truth doesn't come to us through our intellect or emotions. Those are fundamentally flawed as foundations for truth. Truth comes by revelation, and revelation by the Spirit (John 16:13). We know truth because God has revealed himself to us through the Spirit first, then through Scripture, and finally people filled and anointed by the Spirit (2 Timothy 3:16-17).

Truth is also corrective by nature. God didn't send his Son to die and rise from the dead because we have it all figured out. The opposite is true. Truth must correct us, the rod and staff that comforts us and keeps us on the right path (Psalm 23).

The term *to know* means intimacy and oneness, sometimes used in the Scripture for sex, a physical oneness, as in Adam knew Eve. To be made free, we must become one with the truth. Remember, God is truth, not a set of doctrines apart from him (John 14:6).

The bondage resulted from becoming one with a lie, so our freedom must come from joining with the truth.

The root of all sin is a lie, and the Devil is the father of lies (John 8:44). When we live a life of sin, apart from God and in bondage, we are of the Devil's lineage. Since God is truth and life, a lie leads us away from him and into death. The New Covenant sees this problem and fixes it by placing the person of truth within us, transforming us at our most intimate core because God is there.

Now we can be free. Not only with a right to choose, but with the nature that gives us the ability to make choices aligned with God. That's freedom. Greater intimacy with him as a person leads to more and more freedom. God is the highest power, so walking in line with him, following him, means all other authorities break away.

Where the Spirit of the Lord is, there is freedom (2 Corinthians 3:17). Remaining in the Spirit, following close to him, we are free. If the Spirit moves and I stay still, I'm no longer free. When the Spirit remains and I walk my own path, I'm not free.

It's a rule. Actually, it's a law. A good one.

The Law of Liberty

It is more important to be *made* free than *set* free. Being set free still depends on my ability and choices. The Israelites were set free from Egypt, but slavery remained in their hearts. No matter of law (even one from heaven) or shift in geography (even a Promised Land) could change their hearts.

But once we are made free by Christ, we can no longer be made slaves again. Our outward situation can no longer place us in bondage or define our freedom. Think of it like this. If a government can give freedom, then it can also take it away. But inward freedom is based on the power of God and his eternal government, transcendent over all other authority.

But once we are made free by Christ, we can no longer be made slaves again.

Along with the law of spirit and life, the New Testament discusses another law—the law of liberty (James 1:25). Since it is from God, it is a heavenly law, and nothing on earth can suppress it or take it away.

In the classic movie, *Shawshank Redemption*, on cable somewhere at least once a week, we see this theme play out. Andy is innocent of the crime in which he was accused and seeks a way of escape. But Andy was free long before he escaped.

Andy's first day in prison, another newbie inmate dies, and while the hardened prisoners mock and bet on a man's survival, Andy asks the dead man's name. Andy gives dignity. He makes a deal with the guard during a hot work detail, so that they can all drink a cold beer and feel like free men. He redeems and expands the library, giving people purpose and opportunity to read stories happening beyond the gray walls of the prison. Andy locks himself in the warden's office and plays beautiful music through the same loudspeaker that usually oppressed the men.

Andy lives free and teaches others what it means to be free. In prison. He's trying to change their thinking.

It didn't work with everyone, though. Brooks couldn't handle life outside the prison. The prison was within his heart, and he ended up committing suicide.

Red, however, is different. Like Brooks, Red finds it extremely difficult to live *set free*, once he was paroled. But Red listens to Andy's final instructions. Those instructions were the culmination of Red's relationship with Andy, the one who was free from within, and Red joins Andy in paradise.

Being *made* free is the greater freedom.

The law of liberty is higher than any law of any government, any prison-type context in this world. Jesus said, "No one can take my life from me. I sacrifice it voluntarily. For I have the authority to lay it down when I want to and also to take it up again. For this is what my Father has commanded." (John 10:18) His confession before Pilate continually declared a higher authority, his Father (John 18:36). Paul and Silas sang while in prison because they were free from within (Acts 16:25-34). Out of love for the guard, they could stay within the fallen prison walls. They were never really prisoners.

I don't mean to excuse or justify oppression. Not in any way. It's evil. But worldly oppression and tyranny are temporary and subject to change, as are any laws or systems that allow or limit people to live free and complete. Situational freedom can't change the heart. Inward freedom is eternal and of an incorruptible Spirit. No one can stop or enslave a heart that is free in Christ.

Even the grave couldn't hold Jesus. Even death couldn't keep him down.

Renewing Our Minds

We may not feel free. In fact, we often don't. We can confess to feeling weak and useless, and in our own strength, that is true.

But the freedom God provides isn't dependent upon us. Thank God. The freedom of God rests in God alone, and he has placed freedom within us through the Spirit.

To live free, we must renew our minds to what God has done. Our thoughts and feelings are important, but they do not define us anymore. The Devil will lie to us and tell us we are slaves to our feelings, but in Christ, my thoughts and feelings are a part of me, but not my identity. Now armed with the person of truth, we have the spiritual might and power to "cast down imaginations and every high thing that exalts itself against God, bringing into captivity every thought unto the obedience of Christ." (2 Corinthians 10:15)

It seems counter-intuitive, but real freedom is complete obedience to and reliance upon the person of God.

Renewing our minds can't be by our own power and ability. It's not about being intelligent or smart enough to understand. God did the work here, too. Just as he gave his Spirit for us to flow within and live from, he has given us the mind of Christ (2 Corinthians 2:16). The thinking of Jesus is already ours. We simply submit our thoughts to his.

The point isn't to feel bad about what we think or feel, but to realize they have no power over us. Instead, we compare and contrast our thoughts and feelings to the Spirit, who leads us into all truth. Then we align our thoughts to truth in the mind of Christ through the Spirit. There is nothing we think or feel that the Spirit doesn't have an answer for, a correction back to life.

Exploration

How do we discipline our thoughts according to truth? Constant communication with the Spirit, reading and studying scripture, prayer, praise, and the teaching of the Word in community are a few, which we will talk about in more detail later.

I've lost weight recently. 80 pounds. It didn't happen overnight, as we all know. Over time, I stayed consistent with my exercise and eating healthy. There's no quick fix, and it was difficult. I didn't see changes at first, but I stuck with it. Soon I had lost twenty pounds, then thirty, and I could see more progress as I felt years younger and had more energy. I had been transformed.

The core discipline is fixing our mind on an awareness of God's presence. Brother Lawrence's *The Practice of the Presence of God* is a beautiful book along these lines. He shares how he intentionally kept his focus on God through everyday tasks.

I call it the discipline of relationship. I run thoughts and feelings by God, and I ask him what he thinks of people and situations. God is always there, speaking and listening. Develop that awareness and constant conversation. I've even known people who refuse to say, "Amen," when they pray, since the connection never ends.

Father, thank you for making us free. Help us bring all our thoughts and feelings into alignment with the truth that continues to make us free and live accordingly. Amen.

Chapter 15
Rest and Purpose

Vacations are awesome. People share memes about how they need to go to the beach or their dream cabin in the mountains next to a bubbling brook. "I need a break!" When they're on vacation, we get pics with toes in the sand and a drink and a book. "I needed this," they say.

My wife and I were missionary teachers in 2003, and Spring Break approached. A group of young teachers, married and single, met together and planned a trip to Australia. Excited about snorkeling, beaches, and exploring a different county, we started saving money. We didn't get our tickets yet, however, because the travel agents serving the local US military base were great at getting deals last minute.

God changed our plan. It's what he often does. Another teacher mentioned a family serving as missionaries in Fiji, people the local church in Korea supported, yet no one had visited. "Would you guys be willing to go to Fiji instead and visit them?"

The Spirit of God was so clear, I'm not sure we had much of a choice. The answer was a quick *yes*. We changed our vacation into a mission trip. Within a week and a half, we raised money, and bought chain saws to help with damage to the village from a recent tropical storm. More people decided to join us. We went to Fiji and returned with full hearts and more joy than we could have ever received in Australia.

Not there's anything wrong with Australia. It just wasn't where God wanted us to be.

For my wife and me, God changed our idea of vacation. We stopped thinking about where to go for *fun* when we had time off. We started thinking and praying, "God, where do you want us to go?" Instead of vacations, we went on adventures.

Way more fun. Exponentially more joy.

We don't need a break from the mission and purpose of God.

We don't need a break from the mission and purpose of God. To think we do reveals worldly thinking, not a kingdom perspective.

In Fiji, we still had a great time. We swam in a perfectly clear lagoon, followed a stream up a mountain. Everywhere around us looked like a postcard. On another Spring Break trip to India, we preached and led worship, but we also laughed hard and pet elephants.

Sometimes the adventures were difficult and tiring, but the joy and peace of knowing we're on adventure with God and one another makes up for it.

I'm not saying we never need rest, sleep, or downtime. Often, that is what God tells us. "Get away and rest in the mountains for a couple of days." He's a good Daddy and wants what is best for us. He's not impressed with activity for its own sake.

But we only need a break from the Kingdom if we're trying to live heaven on earth in our own strength. Heaven, the purpose and mission of God, it only works by his power, and there's no limit to that. I get tired and broken when I think I need to accomplish something to enjoy peace and rest.

From Peace

The rule of the Kingdom is this–we can't work to get peace. We move and live *from* it.

Everything in our world teaches a way to get peace. We work our jobs and can't wait until closing time or the weekend, taking advantage of our free time to do the things that make us happy. Now we can be at peace. But then we get up and work another day. Or perhaps we think of war, fighting and getting through a conflict until someone wins or there's another type of resolution. Then peace happens. But conflicts can start all over the next day.

Again, our idea of peace or rest is largely situational. We never really get there. We never arrive.

In the Kingdom, we have been given peace, too. Jesus gives peace, but not like the world (John 14:27). His peace isn't dependent upon a situation or physical reality. It is eternal and unchangeable. It is a peace that can't be shaken, and no one can take away. What a gift.

Just like love, righteousness, freedom, and truth, God is peace. Jesus is the Prince of Peace (Isaiah 9:6).

God is simultaneously at complete peace and fully active. He is always at rest and always working, at the same time, both at once. This is impossible in this world, in our strength. They're opposites. But just as light is a wave and a particle, God is both still and active. Jesus never ran or hurried anywhere. He sat when he taught. And yet John tells us that if he wrote down everything Jesus said and did, the world couldn't contain the books (John 21:25).

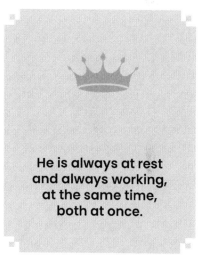

He is always at rest and always working, at the same time, both at once.

That's a lot of activity for a man who walked, sat, and went away by himself to pray every day, *as was his custom.*

Since we've been made free, partakers of the divine nature, then we live by the same reality. When we rest in him, find our peace within God, then what we do has more impact than we thought possible.

Called According to the Purpose of God

He called Lazarus' name and called him to do something.

Jesus didn't wave his hands or speak a spell or do a little dance. Of course, if his Father had required it, he would have. But he didn't.

Every act and word of God has value, meaning, and power. Out of all the possible religious statements or activities Jesus could have done, it is important to notice what he did do.

He called Lazarus by name. Personally. Then Lazarus walked out of the tomb, a living, breathing miracle.

But he didn't just call his name. He gave a command. "Come forth!" It was a call forward to a new life, a life of meaning, purpose, and mission.

We were reborn to live with God, and God is passionately engaged in his purpose, to reconcile all things back to himself through Jesus.

All of his action and interaction with the world, all of his words and plans, for each individual, community, nation, all of creation, is under this simple yet profoundly eternal purpose. He's bringing all of it back into relationship with him.

If we are going to be in a relationship with him, we must be where he is, on his mission and purpose. To be separate from God's mission is to be separate from him. With him is rest, peace, and activity overflowing with meaning. Eternal meaning. That is true for everyone, not only professional ministers, the extremely educated, or charismatic people. That's the life to which we've been individually and corporately called.

Living in the Purpose

God spoke, "Let there be light," and there was light. Then he stepped back a bit and said, "Hey, that's awesome." His own work pleased him.

In the same way, God's purpose pleases him (Ephesians 1:5). He's not reconciling all of creation back to himself through Jesus because he feels obligated to do it, because some standard apart from himself dictates it, or even just to be nice. No. The Father reconciles and redeems all things because it gives him supreme joy. He sings over us (Zephaniah 3:17), he's so happy to be in a relationship with us again, for us to be aligned with our design out of oneness with him. We see this joy in the father's happiness when he sees the prodigal son a long way off.

Just as our unity with him in the Spirit of Christ brings us righteousness and peace, our participation in his purpose brings us joy.

Despite how hard life can be, it's an eternal joy belonging to God. It's an abundant joy to the full that can't be contained or taken from us.

Many will attempt to steal God's joy from us. The Devil, the world, our own sin nature, all of it will resist our participation in the creative, redemptive purpose of God. Painfully so, which is why we've also been called to suffering, to persecution, and grief over the brokenness of this world. But only for a time.

Every tear will be wiped away (Revelation 21:4), every wound healed, every pain and temptation gone, and all that will remain is that which is of Christ (1 Corinthians 3:13-15). There will be a new heaven, and a new earth, and we will enjoy the eternal spectacle and experience of joy and love. We'll have purpose there, too. We will help rule and reign that new place.

That is our inheritance.

Exploration

> *"All who are weary and carry heavy-laden, come to me and I will give you rest. My yoke is easy and my burden is light."* (Matthew 11:28-30)

Jesus makes this statement, and it seems contradictory. I mean, I get tired. We all do. I am ready for some rest. Yes, Jesus, we come to you for rest.

And then we get a yoke and a burden? What is that about?

The words matter. We give up our burden and yoke and the one we get instead belongs to God. A yoke is placed around a neck to pull a wagon or plow, and a burden is a weight. We get God's rest when walking on purpose with him.

But the yoke of God is also attached to him. It is shared with the Father. He doesn't leave us alone to work that yoke. We're walking next to him, and he does the work. That's where the rest is, yoked with him.

A burden is another term for a prophecy, as in, *the burden of the Lord*, like an oracle or a word given to people. That also belongs to God, not us, and we are to speak his words while participating in his work.

This makes sense when we realize that in the economy of God, his rest and activity coexist and happen together, hand in hand.

Father, thank you for giving us rest and peace that come from a source we can't ever lose but must trust in and work from. Thank you for including us in the intimacy of where you are, in purpose, which is where we find our own life and joy. Amen.

Chapter 16
The Eternal Inheritance

My grandmother had been fading for years, and we all knew the end was near. While Grandmother was still aware and coherent, she started telling people to put names on things in her house that we wanted to have when she died, and my aunts continued to encourage us to get a piece of tape, write our name down, and claim the stuff to which we had emotional attachments.

I never could. Not because I thought it was bad in any way. Some people find comfort in having those items from a loved one–a picture that hung in a bedroom or a lamp. I don't really think that way; it's not my *love language,* I guess.

When she passed, they asked for one child from each of the five families to get up and say something at the funeral. Big shock, I was chosen from among my brother and sisters. I stood and spoke, explaining why I never put my name on anything. "But here I am, looking out over a huge family of amazing people that love each other. I want to put my name on that. I want to claim getting to the end of my life and seeing that legacy, a family that loves God and each other. But here's the thing. That's big enough that we can all put our names on it."

My opportunity to get some of Grandmother's possessions was based on one fact. I was her grandchild, the son of her daughter. The bloodline passed down to me. By that connection and identity, I had access to Grandmother's stuff.

It is similar with God.

Children of the King

Being born of God, we are his children. All of humanity is a special creation made in his likeness and image and greatly loved, but humanity isn't begotten of God. When we enter Christ through the blood and resurrection, we become born of his nature, a new creation, a child of God.

As his children with his nature, we also receive an inheritance as sons and daughters of the King (Ephesians 1:11). He recognizes the identity of his Son within us each as individuals and among the whole collective Church. We are called co-heirs with Christ (Romans 8:17).

We sang the song when I was a kid, and I didn't understand the old language, even though we read the KJV all the time. "I'm so glad I'm a part of the family of God … joint heirs with Jesus as we travel this sod …" My first idea of *joint* wasn't exactly church-friendly, and I had no clue what *sod* was. I later understood those powerful words.

The older child within the story of the prodigal son broke my heart and challenged my thinking. At some point, we all feel like the prodigal. We have gone far from God, even if only in our hearts, and must be received back to him in love as full sons and daughters. Moving forward in our faith, many also feel like the older son. He wouldn't go celebrate the return of his brother. Why? Because he felt slighted. He had never been given a fatted calf and a party.

The father corrects the older son. "All that I have is yours. It's always been yours. You could have had a fatted calf and a party with your friends anytime you wanted."

The prodigal son wasted his inheritance and assumed it was mercy to be considered his father's servant, which also had to be corrected. But the older son lived in the house, a full owner of all that wealth, and still thought like a servant.

Most of us, if we're honest, feel the same. We can repeat the phrases and doctrine about being co-heirs with Christ all we want, but we often think and act like servants instead of sons and daughters with full rights and access to heaven. All while living in the house.

Our inheritance is secure (1 Peter 1:4). If God secures it for his children, we can't lose it and can trust in it absolutely. An example of this is when Paul speaks of the hardship of material lack, yet he next declares his ownership of everything (2 Corinthians 6:10). Even when he seemed to own nothing, he rested in the truth that he had access to the resources of heaven.

We question our inheritance because the Devil lies to us. We feel it's too big or our pride wants to earn it. Additionally, we are surrounded by lack, poverty, and limited resources. It takes revelation and the renewal of our mind to consider and trust in a Kingdom with unlimited resources.

What will we ultimately inherit in Christ? A new heaven and earth (Revelation 21).

We aren't in competition with anyone because the inheritance of God is infinite. We each get it in full.

Just as the world was placed under corruption by humanity through the first Adam, all creation will be made new through our being made new first. Creation waits for us to live heaven on earth, to be new creations, because we are the forerunners of a redeemed creation. All has been accomplished through Christ.

Duirng our inevitable times of trouble and heartache, this is our hope. We were once hopeless and in despair and now we have hope, a secure inheritance in Christ. This hope is absolute and unchangeable.

The inheritance of God leads us to peace. We aren't in competition with anyone because the inheritance of God is infinite. We each get it in full. Divide infinity by two and we both get infinity. Divide by 100 and we each get the same as we did before.

Rewards

Just like light is a wave and particle, and we are human and divine, we are heirs of an eternal inheritance and can add to it at the same time.

My friend Rolando says, "Generosity is the currency of the Kingdom." When we give and bless, we get more in eternity. During a teaching to the masses (Luke 12), Jesus reveals how we increase our bank account in heaven by selling what we have and giving to the poor.

Another mind-blowing statement is, "If you receive a prophet as one who speaks for God, you will be given the same reward as a prophet." (Matthew 10:41) In the economy of heaven, blessing a person with something as simple as a cup of water, *and* doing it with the eternal reality in mind (that person has a spiritual gift and role), then we get a reward equal to the prophet.

Further, if we bless another with a cup of water because they are a fellow disciple, Jesus teaches we can't lose the reward (Matthew 10:42). Acting like heaven is more real than what we see builds eternal wealth no one can take away. It doesn't rust. Thieves can't get to it. The government can't even tax it.

Why build wealth on earth where we can't help but lose it all? That's ridiculous when we realize we've been given an opportunity to store things in the Kingdom that we will enjoy forever.

Some will get more than others, according to the parable of the talents. The simple expectation is to invest what the master gave them. And when they obeyed, they enjoyed multiplication, which is the nature of the Kingdom. Then, all the money they received from the investments was given to them. The original talents and power to multiply them wasn't theirs, but since they participated in the process, they ended up owning the results. Oh, what love of a Father.

The one who hid the talent, didn't participate in the process, lost everything.

The parable of talents in Luke goes further. The master gives the good servants rule over cities. (Luke 19:11-27)

Which makes sense. As children of the King, princes and princesses of God, we will rule and reign with him.

To Rule and Reign with Him

Don't you know you're going to rule angels? (1 Corinthians 6:3)

Paul was frustrated with the church in Corinth. They were bickering and divisive. Paul argues they should be able to solve disagreements because of their future role in heaven. One day, in the full Kingdom, we will rule over angels. We don't need the courts of this world to keep us from being divided. On the contrary, we are being trained to rule with Christ and have the power and authority to live united in love with our brothers and sisters.

Jesus tells the disciples they will all rule at his side, despite the selfish way they asked who was going to sit where. He explained they would achieve an authority in the coming Kingdom through suffering and dying to self (Matthew 20:20-28).

We talk and sing about getting crowns in heaven, and it's true, but it should sober us to remember they crowned Jesus with thorns and put a declaration of his kingship on the instrument of his death. No servant is greater than his or her master, Jesus says. They hated him, they'll hate us, too (John 15:20).

For the joy set before him, reconciliation between God and all creation, Jesus endured the cross (Hebrews 12:2). The cross was the path to resurrection and glory. It is the same with us.

If we are to learn what it means to rule with Christ, it will not be by controlling others and ordering them around. That's not how Jesus did it. Paul teaches we should have the same mind as Christ did, submitting as a servant in love and then given a name above all names (Philippians 2).

We won't *get ahead* in the Kingdom using the world's ways and methods. The Son of God leaves us with the formula. If you want to be great, be the servant. If you want to be the greatest, be a slave. Many who are first in this life will be last in the next. And many at the end of the table in this life will be called to the most prominent position by the master at the great feast.

> **If we are to learn what it means to rule with Christ, it will not be by controlling others and ordering them around. That's not how Jesus did it.**

God is a good father, the only good one. And he is training and discipling us to rule with him in eternity through humility, self-sacrifice, and service to others in love. It's not easy, but it is the way.

Exploration

Service is not a gift of mine. I don't naturally think of ways to serve others.

Yet that isn't an excuse, not if Christ, the ultimate Servant, lives within me. I'm called to serve, despite my personality.

I have been fortunate to be in community with people who flow with service like a fish in water. It amazes me. I've learned from them, watching them, seeing how they act and love people. I've emulated those with the gift of service and become better at recognizing the opportunities and listening to the Spirit. God has been so kind to nudge me to notice people, see their needs and show me ways to *give a cup of cold water*. Not because I'll get anything from people in return, but because it pleases my Father and gives me treasure in heaven.

We serve and give because what we have in Christ is secure. With the resources of heaven, giving to others out of love and service takes nothing from me. If anything, it adds to my eternally secure account.

Is service your gift? Share it with the church community, inviting others along with you. We all need to learn it.

Do you know someone with the gift of service? It's obvious once you think about it and ask God to show you. Follow them around and take note of what they do.

It's a worthy discipline, full of rewards both here and later.

Father, we praise you for passing on an inheritance that we can't lose in heaven and eternal resources here and now as your child. Teach us how to rule and reign with you through serving others as Christ did, with his Spirit and love. Amen.

Chapter 17
The New People

A different race of beings with powers, like humans, but not.

Beginning in the 60s and created by Stan Lee, the X-men were a group of teenagers with new abilities based on a mutation that gave them powers. But they didn't simply exist with those powers. The mutant teens gathered into a superhero team to help people and fight evil. Professor X helped them navigate the new mutant life.

It's a fun story with complex themes about how we all feel like misfits at some point. Stan Lee clearly expressed how he wanted to show the evils of racism and hate.

We won't go into the scientific issues of the X-men here—how mutations are almost always harmful, if not in every case. The comic series developed to explain mutants were a new race of people, the next stage of evolution.

The Old Testament lineage was physical, and the redemptive ancestry of Jesus is traced for us twice in the Gospels. In Luke, his ancestry is traced back to Adam and in Matthew, back to Abraham. The Messianic covenant and promise through David were physical—Jesus would be born of David's kingly line (2 Samuel 7).

But after Jesus, the New Testament doesn't trace a physical family. It has a lineage, though, a new one based on the Spirit, through discipleship and mentorship, the passing on of the things of the Father. This lineage traces Jesus to Peter and the apostles. The apostles to Barnabas. Barnabas to Paul. Paul to Timothy, all the way down to us. We are part of a new lineage that traces faith across two thousand years.

And yet, wonder of wonders, while there are a thousand generations between us and Jesus, I am born of God just like Peter, Paul, and Barnabas. We are all direct descendants of the Father, not great-great grandchildren to the 100th degree.

Being reborn, we are no longer completely human. We may appear human, but we are born of another world. Our birth from the Father is individual based on our repentance, and at the same time, we are now interconnected with a whole new race of people, the children of God across two thousand years, each begotten of God through the One Spirit.

Scripture explores the many implications of this. We will discuss three.

New Family

We were once not a people, but now through Christ, we are
(1 Peter 2:10).

It shouldn't surprise us that God models the church after the family.

God is, within himself, a family. Father, Son, Holy Spirit. His model for redemption is an expression of himself, a family. The Garden of Eden was perfect, and humanity hadn't yet sinned, when God gave Adam and Eve the command to spread his creative order across the earth through family. Adam and Eve disobeyed God and cast creation into corruption. As the people of the world became more violent toward one another, the opposite purpose of family, God used another family, Noah's, as a mode of redemption and salvation.

Again, humanity decided to try to get to heaven their own way, but the Tower of Babel was not the way people would get to God.

What was God's solution after Babel? God called a man with a wife and told them they would have a host of ancestors that would bless all people. That necessitated a child, a son, which also became part of the promise.

God could have sent his Son an infinite number of ways, but he chose to send Christ into a family, born of Mary and adopted by Joseph.

Being in Christ and Christ in us, we are now within the family trinity.

My background is Irish and German, and I was born in America. That cultural identity wasn't lost entirely when I entered that radical saving relationship with God, but I did have to die to it as my primary identity. My earthly labels and source died with me in Christ on the cross, but they were also redeemed into something new.

The view of heaven we get in Revelation is of countless people surrounding the throne, worshipping God. They are all different languages and tongues, a picture of the unity and diversity we desire. We see the same at the first manifestation of the Spirit of God on the Day of Pentecost. The one message of God's glory expressed through languages people could understand was a redemption of that ancient tower of Babel.

In Christ, the divisions have ceased, and our first identity is in him, not any earthly nationality or background.

This places us in a new family. I now have brothers and sisters across the street, across the world, across centuries, and they are more related to me than my own earthly family. This challenges us, but I am more family with a person across the world who is born of God than with a sibling who isn't a Christian, because the family of the Spirit will last beyond this life.

My role as son, brother, husband, and father, are all temporary. Jesus explains my marriage won't last into eternity (Matthew 22:30). My children won't be my kids, and so forth. God cares about those relationships and expects me to express the Kingdom through family responsibilities. I am to love my wife (Ephesians 5), honor my parents, and raise my children in truth. But as important as those roles are, they are only temporary. To remain in an eternal relationship with the people I love, they must also become part of the forever family through Christ.

Fortunately, much of my earthly family follows the Lord. My

parents, wife, siblings, and kids become my brothers and sisters in God when they choose to follow him. That will remain, and in heaven I will only know them as co-heirs in Christ.

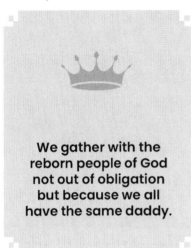

We gather with the reborn people of God not out of obligation but because we all have the same daddy.

We are a new people from a new source, Jesus, the Father, and the Spirit instead of Adam. We are a new race of beings from another world and only visiting this one. As previously discussed, God's model for redemption is the family, and the Church is modeled after the family. The Church isn't an organization, she's an organism, given family terms like *the bride*.

Periodically, my parents send out a message for when the Mooney family will meet, and even though we are all unique in our own way, we show up. There's a place set for each of us for one simple reason—we're family, from the same lineage and name. It matters.

We gather with the reborn people of God not out of obligation but because we all have the same daddy. Gathering with one another is a declaration of a greater reality, something eternal and invisible but more real than what we see. Through other aliens and strangers, we come together to encourage each other on this walk of heaven on earth, reminding one another of what is eternally true. Therefore, as Hebrews says, don't give up meeting together (Hebrews 10:25). That would be rejecting our family and cutting ourselves off from our primary identity as children of the King.

Again, this is a work of God, finished and done in Christ. We can't manufacture the unity and the family of God. Neither can we decide who our brothers and sisters are. That's Daddy's decision (John 1:13). We must learn from the Spirit how to walk in the reality of our family unity in God, which takes some dying to self and sacrifice, but the blessing of unity is powerful and worth it.

While we fellowship as a family when we gather, hanging out isn't the only goal. We get together with our family to train for the war we're facing.

New Army

The X-men wear uniforms and gather at a school to learn about life but also how to use their powers for good. Then they are sent from the Xavier School to fight against evil and to help people.

The gathering has a purpose: to be trained and sent out to our different contexts, empowered and encouraged to live heaven on earth.

We have an enemy that does all he can to steal, kill, and destroy. Each individual, local faith community, and the church are targets for his schemes and attacks. Many Christians act as if they've been invited by Christ onto a cruise ship. Then they are surprised and discouraged when they quickly experience the truth—they've been recruited on to a battleship (1 Peter 4:12).

> **Make no mistake. We're in a war for the eternal souls of every living man and woman.**

Trying to continue like our local gatherings are a country club leaves us open to attack and division, due to our ignorance, willing or not.

Make no mistake. We're in a war for the eternal souls of every living man and woman, our own included.

Even when we start to understand this, we are beset by another lie from the Devil–that we are alone in the fight. But we aren't alone. We have a family that has our backs. We weren't meant to fight alone, but alongside a family.

Family is a force when we fight together, and that goes for both our earthly and heavenly ones. We segregate along ages and interests in our churches and wonder why people aren't growing and stepping up to the task. The family was meant to grow and serve on mission together, not separated from each other.

The same is true for the local church family. Remember our need for intimacy and purpose? We see the same here. We do more together. Where two or more are gathered, where two or more agree, one defeats a thousand and two ten thousand. Together in Christ is where the power is found.

There's one more reason we fight as part of the family of God. Our weapons aren't force, coercion, and intimidation. We fight with the love that never fails (1 Corinthians 13), through service, sacrifice, and dignity of all people. Healing, not hurting. Families are the result of love, and love is our greatest weapon against the evil of the world and hell.

God is three in one, and we reveal who he is by living his purpose with two or more in oneness. If we reveal our identity as the people of God through loving one another, then we must be sent with others. Jesus sent them out by two. God called Paul and Barnabas, and they brought Mark with them. This army of love reveals the Kingdom to a broken and hurting world.

New Temple

In the Old Testament, God gave Solomon the commission to build a temple. Modeled after the Mosaic Tabernacle, it became the resting place of the physical representation of God's presence, the Ark of the Covenant.

There's much we could say about the Old Testament Tabernacle and Temple, but they were shadows and symbols of what God was going to do through the New Covenant. The New Testament never commissions building a physical structure. On the contrary, one of Paul's messages in Acts states God doesn't live in buildings made with human hands (Acts 17:24). Where does he live, then?

Within his people. The New Testament expresses that we, as the church, are the house of God now (1 Peter 2:5). Each individual is also a temple of God through the Holy Spirit, but the majority of the passages about the temple in the New Testament speak of us collectively as his home.

Christ was the first living stone, and the cornerstone with which we align (Ephesians 2:20-22). We are each like him, living stones God uses to build his house, the place where he lives.

The Old Testament Tabernacle no longer exists. It has rotted away. Solomon's Temple is dust. All that's left of the rebuilt temple in Jerusalem is the Wailing Wall. A new temple built with stones of this world would have the same problem. If it has a beginning, it will have an end.

The new temple spoken of in the New Testament is an eternal one, and an eternal house must be built with eternal materials. That's us. We've been made one with the eternal Spirit of God, meaning our spirit has been remade into something that shares the divine nature, without beginning and therefore without end. We are the living stones, eternal stones that make up the eternal temple. God's chosen house.

These are stones and not bricks, by the way. There were so many stones in Ireland that they had to remove them to plant crops along the hills. The Irish made walls from the stones, which was a challenge. Bricks are easy. Just pile one on top of the other. Stones must fit just right, one abnormal shape aligning with another.

In the Old Testament, it was against the law to make an altar to God from man-made, cut bricks (Exodus 20:25). Altars had to be made from stones, each one a different shape and size. No two stones were the same. For human hands to manufacture uniform stones, to make them fit, was to pollute and ruin worship.

We aren't bricks but stones, each unique, new creations in Christ, different shapes and sizes but made of the same substance. And God is the grand builder who fits us together to make a beautiful house where he can live forever. We are the New Jerusalem we see descending from heaven, the bride of Christ established as a temple city on the new earth (Revelation 21). That is both on a local and universal church level.

Any attempt to make a physical place holy is either misguided distraction at best, or a lie at the worst. We are the house. He is God with us, Immanuel. God lives in a people. That's who he gave his life to redeem. Living in oneness with the new creation family, and that family with one another, pleases him.

Exploration

I must be intentional to set aside time to go on dates with my wife. The same needs to happen with my kids and extended family. We make it a priority.

We must also make gathering with the family of God a priority in our life, gathering for mutual encouragement through the gifts that God has given us.

Neither my immediate family, nor my extended one, are perfect. Their perfection isn't why I choose to spend time with them. It's the same with the church. No local gathering will be perfect and have all the elements we find important as individuals. That's consumerist thinking.

Ask God to lead you to the right gathering of saints where you can partner in the mission of God and find encouragement. Then show up. And keep showing up.

Father, thank you for giving us a great eternal family to learn more about your love and mission. Show us how to be a sent people with others, not alone, and come alongside local communities to see your miracle and healing spread to the world. Amen.

THREE

FIGHT

Unwrapping the Gift

And the dead man came out, his hands and feet bound in graveclothes, his face wrapped in a headcloth. Jesus told them, "Unwrap him and let him go!" (John 11:44).

Lazarus was dead and now alive, but he waddled out, still wrapped in the grave clothes. Even his face and eyes were covered.

Christ did the work. God raised the dead. Again, Jesus could have walked up and unwrapped the guy, or maybe waved his hand and commanded the cloth to disappear. He didn't. The Son of God called out to the community once more and instructed them.

Unwrap him. Set the new life free.

We repent unto the Father and are now a new creation, unique with gifts, talents, purpose, and more, all within the finished work of Christ.

Yet our mind hasn't been renewed to the truth. Our inward person is regenerated but we still carry over ways of thinking, being, and doing that are left over from our old, dead life. It's a dead life, but it still influences us. The dead ways of thinking, our dead identity, blind us and keep us bound, even though at our core we've been radically changed.

Thus, we begin a process of lifelong transformation where we learn more and more how to live from the new life within us, removing what is dead and revealing what is alive and beautiful.

The Church is the context in which this happens. The gathered family of God, in a local and consistent context, is a necessary component of the transformation process. We need each other to live in our purpose and walk completely free.

Religion, however, in the worldly sense, prefers that we keep on those grave clothes. We're easier to manipulate, control and milk for money. That's not the Jesus Model.

The message of Christ within a family of faith removes the dead that binds, reveals walking miracles, and sends them out into the world.

Yet, we also have an enemy on this journey to reveal the new life within us. All creation groans and waits for the reborn to be revealed, but the Devil is absolutely terrified of reborn children of God joining the Father in purpose and mission. Satan is dedicated to the utmost, with all the resources at his disposal, to keep us from living the truth, to instead live by his lies.

Here is where we FIGHT. We don't fight as the world does, however. We must renew our minds according to the new creation and *fight* from the victory that's already been won in Christ. We discover the gift within and join the mission for the hearts and souls of humanity. That discovery places us in the war. We will fight battles.

When we do, we find who we really are in Christ.

Chapter 18
Discipline of Relationship

At some point, modern medicine offered new, improved ways of having children. The motivation was noble. Women and babies died due to issues with childbirth, many times having the child at home. My grandma complained once about how a relative came to visit while she was laboring in the living room. She felt responsible for entertaining while giving birth.

Advances were made with technology and drugs. Progress included placing the pregnant mother in a bright and sterile room, usually stark white, surrounded by medical professionals like nurses (probably strangers) and doctors (generally a male they had met a few times). Husbands and relatives were out in the waiting room. Pain medication was given to the mother to ease the process. This became the norm and proper for *civilized* people. We even influenced other countries to do the same.

Eventually, research revealed some interesting facts. Births statistically went better for the woman and child without drugs. With husbands and women relatives in the delivery room, mothers were more at ease and less anxious. A dim and quiet room also had a calming effect. They called this *natural* childbirth like it was a revelation.

Thank God for medical progress. My wife trained and served as a *doula* for several births, and a of couple times, medical intervention was necessary. But even modern medicine has had to learn how advantageous love and relationships are to the production of life.

We do the same in the church sometimes. We have bigger buildings and more entertaining worship and programs that pump out the numbers. Churches segregate the young from the old in different services to serve their *needs* and then wonder why we are more and more divided and research the reason young people move on from faith. In addition, through COVID, we've increased our online presence and go to church through social media. There's nothing evil in the methods, necessarily, and they can all be tools, but none of them can take the place of the one thing that makes a difference. Relationships.

When a crisis happens in the life of a Christian, they don't need a better online message. They need family around them.

Relationships matter. There are many statistics about what happens to kids without a father in the home, or disengaged parents. Simply showing up as a father and as parents improves the likelihood of a stable and healthy life for the child.

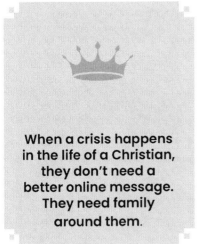

When a crisis happens in the life of a Christian, they don't need a better online message. They need family around them.

The word *relationship* has become overused in evangelical circles, and it's in danger of losing meaning. However, we should explore the importance before we continue, because it is at the core of what we call Christianity.

God is, within himself, a relationship. From his nature, all of creation operates out of relationship. There is relationship between the galaxies within the universe to the solar systems within the galaxy to the planets within the system to the beings and life on the planet to the microscopic cells in the body to the very building block of matter, the atom. It all survives and operates in relation to something else.

Our primary discipline centers on a very simple and absolute idea–our relationship to Christ.

The name Israel means one who wrestles with God. The Lord gave Jacob this name because the patriarch clung to God and wouldn't let go until God blessed him. Jacob's transformation resulted from that central principle. He stuck with God and wouldn't let go (Genesis 32:24-32). It is the same with us.

The Simplicity of Christ

"It's complicated."

Facebook had a place once where you could list your relationship status. Single. Married. Dating. One option was, "it's complicated."

The Christian life isn't complicated. It's simple. Difficult, definitely. But simple.

Paul worries about the church in Corinth. He fears the Corinthians were being led away in their minds with the same sin as Eve (1 Corinthians 11:3-4). Led away from what? The simplicity that is in Christ. This is Paul, who writes some seriously mystic and philosophical statements and builds arguments over several chapters. But he's concerned. Don't be led away like Eve.

How like Eve? Eve already had it all. She came into the perfect and complete realm of Eden with God and Adam. Eve had intimacy and a purpose. She walked with God and did what he said. The Devil convinced her maybe there was something more.

There's not. There's nothing more than God. Simple.

We like complication, however. It makes us feel smart, intelligent, and feeds our pride. If it's complicated, we can use special words and get master's degrees and doctorates in it and now we know more than other people and can get positions in organizations ... it keeps going.

But if it's simple, then we're all on equal ground. Every person needs Christ. It's all him. Reading through the first chapters of Ephesians, Paul continually uses prepositions. Prepositions are words like *with, of, from, in,* and they show relationship. Read through those first 3 chapters and notice how often he relates everything back to the Father, Christ, and the Spirit.

Simple doesn't mean easy. If I say, "Go jump off that building and fly to the moon." That's a simple statement, but not easy. It's extremely difficult or even impossible. That's why we need a new nature and the power of the Spirit to even do a simple thing like to remain in relationship with Christ.

Simple isn't *simplistic*. Simple can be infinitely deep and complex. "I love you" can be cliché, but between two people at the right moment in the proper context, that same statement can possess decades of stories and meaning.

Our discipline is a singular focus on Christ. Everything that matters, anything that has value, flows from him.

Maturity in Christ

Simple doesn't mean we don't mature. There's a process of transformation we've already mentioned of removing the dead thinking and revealing what is truth and life.

1 John 2 mentions three levels of maturity when writing to the church. First, John addresses little children, marked by the realization their sins have been forgiven. Second, he speaks to young people because they have overcome the Devil.

Then he communicates to fathers and mothers in the faith. What marks them? They walk with God. That's pretty simple. They just walk with God. When he moves, they move. When he stops, they stop. That's maturity.

Those first two steps can't be skipped, though. We need the stage of realizing the work of God in forgiveness, his love and mercy. We need the stage of *fighting* with God, realizing our power and our purpose in him. We need to be trained in these new abilities by going through tough situations and overcoming by faith and the Spirit. Both levels teach us more in depth about who God is.

But maturity, the ultimate goal, is simply walking with the Father.

Guess who knows best how to remove those dead clothes that bind us? Christ. No one removed his grave clothes when he rose from the dead. He did that himself. They were folded nicely in the empty tomb when he exited that grave (John 20:7).

I'll repeat it here. Jesus only said what he heard the Father say and only did what he saw the Father do. Simple. Can I get more mature than Jesus? Of course not. He's the goal.

Our Goal for Others

Does this mean we don't need the Body of Christ? Absolutely not. It is the Christ in others through relationship, love, and the gifts of the Spirit that helps remove those grave clothes and call to the deep miracle within us.

This simplicity also defines our relationship with others. It isn't only for pastors, ministry leaders, or someone with a title. Every one of us has influence and leadership in someone's life around us. How should we use that leadership?

Plead with them to be relationally reconciled to God. And once reconciled, continually encourage them to listen to the Spirit and walk with the Father through Christ. Yes, we tell stories and spend time and meet needs, but there's no greater agenda than to lead others to Jesus, to see him better, to love him more. That is the most loving thing we can do for ourselves and others.

Guess who knows best how to remove those dead clothes that bind us? Christ.

The New Testament encourages us to continue to gather, but even more so, the writers in the New Covenant want to make sure we are in Christ more than we are in church. Because the greater includes the lesser. When we are in Christ, we are in the Body of Christ, and he will lead us to gather with the God family. Guaranteed.

The Bible uses three words for Jesus, and they aren't interchangeable-Lord, Jesus, and Christ. Lordship deals with authority and power and government. Jesus is Yeshua, salvation, the one who died and rose again, God in human form, leading to forgiveness and mercy.

Christ is the eternal nature of God, the anointing of both King and Priest, the power to will and do the pleasure of God. The New Testament writers' primary concern was for people to be in Christ, the eternal anointing, because all life and goodness flow from him.

Paul and the other writers in the New Testament use those terms on purpose. Collectively, we are the body of Christ, the expression of the King of heaven here on earth.

What should we talk about when we gather? Let us preach the message and Good News of Christ to one another, and that will draw out the new life from all who hear it, deep calling unto deep (Psalm 42:7).

Exploration

Jesus went into the wilderness to pray, *as was his custom*. He needed to pull away and connect with his Father. He remained connected throughout the day, but that constant communication worked alongside the times he met with the Father in secret.

My friend and mentor Chris has learned to start the day by resting in the mercy of God. The Father's mercies are new every morning, and Chris begins his day with an acknowledgement of who God is and the utter reliance upon God's grace and mercy, which is different from a devotional. Devotionals can be good, but whatever we do must be within relationship.

How do you pull away and listen? How do you make sure you practice hearing his voice?

Father, the simple truth is that it is all about you. You alone are good and real and loving. Help us make you our focus, always listening and asking for your input in every decision and situation. Amen.

Chapter 19
The Power of Community

Children are born with potential and promise. Parents look at their little bundles of awesome and begin to imagine a person who is about to change the world and do great things. We believe.

I was no different when my kids were born. I have three, the oldest is a boy and then two girls. As parents, we teach and train them to make good choices and do what is right, to have character. However, we can take that too far when we try to force their lives along a certain path.

Thankfully, I prayed a great deal over my children when they were in the womb. I prayed they would hear God's voice and love him with all their hearts and lead a life that glorified him. Those prayers shifted my thinking. God can do more than I imagine, so while the character and foundation of truth are important, I had to take a discovery attitude with who each of my kids are.

First, I assume they're not like me. In ways, they will be, but they are individuals with talents and a calling on their life I don't have. Next, I listen and pay attention. What do they like and don't like? Are they introverts or extroverts? What are they good at doing?

Here's the problem. What if my daughter wants to be a mechanic? What if that brings her joy, and she's creative with it? I'm no expert on engines, so she won't learn to work on cars directly from me nor my wife. But God has given a solution to the problem. The Church. There are people in our local fellowship and larger network of Christians that love Jesus and work as mechanics. My daughter can then learn from others how to be a disciple of Christ who happens to be a mechanic.

In a discovery attitude, my wife and I can't be the only examples of what it means to be lovers of Jesus. Yes, we are the primary example of hearing God and doing what he says for our kids. But beyond our influences, my kids need to see other diverse possibilities of what disciples can look like. Thank God we have those amazing people in our natural and spiritual familes.

It's the same in the church. When a believer comes into our midst, it is the community's joy to make no assumptions about the gifts and talents but instead discover and call out the amazing new creation within them, support the gifts, and encourage them.

As we see in the narrative of Lazarus, we as a spiritual family are instrumental in the Jesus Model of revealing the new life of God in others so they can live heaven on earth.

The Outpost of Heaven

Adam and Eve were created in the image of God and placed within Eden, an outpost of heaven on earth, so they could see the model and replicate it. The Tabernacle and the Temple in Jerusalem had elements of that, too, the place of God's presence, meeting with God in a symbolic heaven on earth.

Jesus didn't build a physical structure while on earth. He gathered a group of disciples and followers and taught them about the Kingdom and the love of the Father. In Acts, the apostles brought together the thousands of new converts into a new, strange community.

Think about it. There were twelve leaders that had no way of personally discipling tens of thousands of people. People met every night from house to house, and they ate together. Sounds like a family (Acts 2:46; 5:42). These new believers also gathered to hear apostolic teaching and yet were trusted to go out and live it without ministerial supervision.

The apostles taught new believers to follow the Spirit and trusted God to do his job. He did. Many individuals had arrived from around the Roman Empire for the Feast of Pentecost and just stayed, living with other disciples. Believers gave of their extra to any in need, and Acts says that no one had lack (Acts 4:34). Every need was provided. Let's not forget the power of God was so evident that others from outside of Jerusalem would come to this new community to get healed (Acts 5:16).

Sounds like heaven on earth to me.

They were persecuted, too (Acts 8), as Jesus was and as he promised would happen.

Our local gatherings of believers should operate as outposts of heaven—communities where people know God lives among them.

Our local gatherings of believers should operate as outposts of heaven—communities where people know God lives among them.

For us to live heaven on earth, we need examples to emulate. The first example is Christ himself. Next, we need the expression of God thorugh others that influence and mentor us. Further, we require a community that lives the culture of heaven as a local family. These aren't separate but meant to work as one.

Hebrews tells us to keep meeting together so we don't get dragged into unbelief (Hebrews 3:12). Unbelief is different than disbelief. Disbelief is saying, "God doesn't exist." Unbelief says, "God exists but won't help me." It was unbelief that kept an entire generation from the Promised Land. Even though they saw God tear down the most powerful kingdom on earth, they looked at the giants in the land and refused to go in (Numbers 13).

Continued participation in the church, the outpost of heaven, keeps us in faith and from unbelief. Of course, our enemy knows this, trying his best to divide us from our spiritual family. He is an accuser, remember, and none of us are perfect, so it is easy to pit people against one another in the church. It is often a fight to stick with the Body of Christ, to forgive, reconcile, show grace and love. However, we need one another. It's worth the fight to love.

A Family of Misfits

God loves misfits. He often starts his epic plans with one. The people God uses were always *too* something. Too old, too young, too poor, or not from the right family, whatever.

The Father uses misfits because the work he's doing doesn't fit in this world. This reality is too limiting. We'll need to think outside of the norm to even get started. Jesus was the ultimate misfit, God in human form, a seemingly impossible unity of man with the divine.

Misfits often feel alone, though. Thinking and living outside the norm separates us from others and creates distance. People don't understand the misfit and rarely accept them.

But in the Kingdom, we're all aliens and strangers here (1 Peter 2:11), actual people from a separate reality. The local and universal church is the one place that should celebrate the strange and the misfit.

The goal isn't even to be a misfit. It's being like Christ, and that will by nature make us aliens and strangers.

Paul tells us to not conform to the ways of this world. But our goal can't be nonconformity, either, because then we're still using the world as the point of reference, just rebelling against it. Nonconformists are actually conforming to the idea of nonconformity, still in the bondage thinking of the world.

The opposite of conforming to this world is to be transformed by the renewing of our mind according to the reality of the kingdom of heaven. Thinking according to heaven frees us from the limits of this world, even its idea of being a misfit, and completely removes this world as any example at all.

The goal isn't even to be a misfit. It's being like Christ, and that will by nature make us aliens and strangers.

As unique as we all are, there is one element that can't be different– the expression of Christ. The DNA of God runs through us all, and we are in his family. That DNA will emerge and manifest through the various parts of the body of Christ.

Who can teach us how to live like aliens and strangers? First,

Christ, then other aliens and strangers in Christ. Think of the countless movies, from sports to superheroes, where a group of *misfits* join forces for a greater cause. It is a universal longing given freely in the church.

The examples we see in the church aren't to be mimicked, though. This isn't about uniformity. If we see a doctor following Christ, then the solution isn't for all of us to become Christian doctors. Paul says, "imitate me as I imitate Christ." (1 Corinthians 4:16) What do we imitate in other disciples? We imitate the ways they imitate Christ. We can be doctors, construction workers, bankers, or from countless other contexts and cultures, but we will be misfits in all of them because our primary culture is the Kingdom. Every family has a culture, and the family of God has one, too, instituted by the Father and carried through generations. Part of God's culture is to accept and appreciate the creative ways that Christ is expressed in individuals and groups.

Sending Out

I'm not training my kids to be good kids. I'm training them to be amazing adults.

I have a long view of training, beyond the moment or their current age. Yes, I want them to behave in certain situations, but who they are becoming on the inside will have an impact far in the future. That's more important.

When my kids were young toddlers, I'd cuddle them close and say, "Can I keep you forever?"

They would first respond, "Yes!"

I'd correct them. "No. I love you very much, but I don't get to keep you forever. One day you will grow up and get a job and have your own house, maybe your own family. But I will always love you, and you'll always be my child."

We are a sent people. That identity comes from the Spirit within us. Jesus was sent from God (John 3:16). The Spirit was sent from Jesus (Acts 2). Jesus sent out the disciples to make more of themselves (John 20:22).

Being a healthy family is empowering the kids to become responsible adults. If my son is 25 and I'm still changing his diaper, there is a serious problem. Either he has a disability, or I've failed as a father.

This is true for the church family, as well. We must teach and empower Christians to be responsible for their own spiritual walk. They need to hear from God themselves and find their individual purpose, gift, and calling. There are too many people who have been Christians for decades that expect a leader to change their spiritual diapers. They need to be weaned off the milk.

A false idea of religion resists empowering people like this. Ministers and leaders like to feel needed. It feeds their ego. I'm telling you as one myself. But that's not the Jesus Model. He left and empowered his disciples with his own nature and Spirit, to follow the Father as children of heaven.

Being *sent* doesn't necessarily mean people leave to other geographical areas, but it might. People being led by the Spirit are like the wind, unseen and a little unpredictable (John 3:8).

Unpredictable doesn't mean unstable. We can't use the idea of *following the Spirit* to be flighty or as an excuse to not be committed, disciplined, or faithful. We must live up to our commitments and our word (Matthew 5:37). God has changed the direction of my life several times, and in every case, I made sure to leave well, finish a contract, etc., before moving forward in the new call.

Following the Spirit also does not entail rejecting the bride of Christ. As we already examined, God sends people together, even if the group is as small as two.

God can change our direction in a moment, and it's nearly impossible to build an earthly organization out of people like that, which is why many leaders resist these ideas. However, the calling isn't to build an organization. It's to spread the family of God out like kudzu across the world. In a family, we want those we love to mature and come into their own places, their own households, and start their own families.

Because their kids will start their own families, and so on and so on. That was the model at creation with Adam and Eve, and it's the redemptive Jesus Model, to live heaven on earth, the reason we have been reborn.

Exploration

In the family of God, we need three types of people in our lives. First, mentor figures, people who pour into us from their experience. Second, we must mentor others, pour into them from what God has placed within us. Third, we need friends, brothers and sisters along our same age and path, people with similar interests. Paul had Barnabas as a mentor. He mentored Timothy and others, teaching them to teach and lead, and still others he called fellow ministers.

Who have been those people over the course of your life? Who are they now? These relationships are absolutely necessary if we are to grow to live heaven on earth. They encourage us in our gift, spur us on to our purpose, and heal us when we are wounded. They correct us back to our calling and identity when we fail. This is the function of the family.

We can't manufacture these relationships, but we can be intentional about seeking them out. If God shows you a person you can learn from, show up where they are. Plan a way to spend time with them. If God reveals someone to pour into, invite them along with things you're doing. Eat meals and reach out to friends in the church and spend time together.

You won't get all of what you need in one person or meeting. Live life with people. Share your homes, families, and lives together. Over time, you will see the value and reap the benefits in all three types of relationships.

Father, thank you for the local gathering of Jesus followers, our family of misfits, aliens and strangers from heaven. We have been born again to fit in heaven, all by your love and grace and mercy through Your Son. Show us the people you'd have us invest in and glean from today. Amen.

Chapter 20
Remove the Old

If it were easy, everyone would do it.

Attributed to the coach in the movie *A League of Their Own*, this quote is often used to inspire people to do great things.

When I tell people I'm an author, or they find out somehow, almost every person says, "Hey, I've got a great idea for a book." Or they have several ideas. A few have started. It is rare for them to have finished one.

Ideas are a dime a dozen, probably cheaper. We all have great ideas and get excited about our own or when we hear a great one. You know what's hard? Execution.

For an author, that means writing in my *spare* time. Authors don't have more time than anyone else. Writing a book is waking up early or staying up late, stealing time when others are out having fun. Writing when we're not working a job or spending moments with family.

Books aren't written quickly, so this is at least a commitment of several months, just for a rough draft. Then comes the hard part. Revision. Editing. Revising again. Figuring out what path to take for publication.

Most people don't get past "I've got this idea …"

The Path of the Cross

The way to life is narrow because it's hard, as Jesus said (Matthew 7:13-14). We hear the Gospel pitch of new life, hope, purpose, and eternity in heaven, and we're like, "Yeah! Sign me up."

Then it gets hard, and people quit. If you've been in church for a while, you've heard the examples in the Parable of the Sower (Matthew 13:1-23) and observed it in action. You see people who jump into this faith and are ready to go one day, but sometime later, they quit on church and God, all for various reasons.

Why? What makes this so difficult?

Two things, and they are interconnected. First, we try to do this supernatural walk in our own natural strength. We'll get tired and discouraged quickly that way.

Second, and this is the underlying issue of the first, we must die to ourselves. Deitrich Bonhoeffer wrote in *The Cost of Discipleship*, "When Christ calls a man, he bids him come and die." Bonhoeffer died for his faith in a concentration camp under Nazi Germany, by the way.

We can't get around it. There is joy, new life, and glory beyond our wildest imagination, but the path there is the cross. Jesus went to the cross in a way we couldn't. He killed death and sin within himself on that gruesome tree. But that doesn't mean we escape the cross. To follow Christ, we must follow him to the cross first.

> **There is joy, new life, and glory beyond our wildest imagination, but the path there is the cross.**

We can't be resurrected, nor live the resurrection life, without being dead first. And choosing it.

There are several scriptures clearly telling us what it takes to follow Jesus–take up our cross daily (Luke 9:23), surrender to the greater king (Luke 14:31), and the Kingdom law states, "if you try to hang on to your life, you will lose it. But if you give up your life for my sake, you will save it." (Matthew 16:25)

When we try to live the life of Christ in our own strength, we are, in essence, seeking to save our own lives, which ends in eternal loss and death. But what are we trying to avoid? Dying to self.

What if Lazarus had fought the men trying to remove the grave clothes from him? What if he had said, "No! This is who I am! These grave clothes are my identity." Maybe the men would have been considered hateful for trying to strip off the dead things that had Lazarus bound. But then, Lazarus would have been waddling around for the rest of his life blind and bound. It is love to call dead things dead and cry out to the new life within.

The apostle Paul preached Christ crucified as a central part of the Gospel (1 Cor 15). Yet, the cross is offensive to Jews and Gentiles, to all humanity. It seems painful or stupid. The cross states that we aren't good or strong enough to save ourselves. We don't want to give up control over our lives and our stuff, so we resist the cross. Even roaches scurry away, trying to escape and live, when I chase them with a shoe. Our very nature is to seek to save ourselves, and yet that way puts the proverbial nail in our eternal spiritual coffin.

Dying to self isn't fun. At all. No one likes it. Not even Jesus. I've never seen a church billboard that says, "Come this Sunday and die to yourself!"

At some point, our Christian culture tried to make church fun. If the lost would gather because it was fun, then maybe they would later come to follow Jesus. We attract people with fun, which may draw large crowds, but then that's what they'll expect from then on, the cruise ship experience. Fun isn't the primary goal of our gathering. It's preparing for the purpose of God with the family of the Father. From that, we get meaning and our deepest needs satisfied, a great joy, and even fun. We can't flip the priorities.

Jesus had horrible marketing, calling people to a gruesome cross and a hard life, which Paul also did in his ministry.

Yet Jesus didn't call people to die because he wanted to hurt them. No, he called them through death to self to greater love and eternal life. Many people stopped following him due to this message, but that narrow way produces actual disciples, not cultural Christians.

If we are to follow Jesus in the joy of amazing resurrection life, then we willingly climb up on that oppressive and painful cross with him. There's no other way.

Dying by the Spirit

If you haven't noticed the theme by now, here it is again. We can't even die to ourselves in our own strength. Managing the weakness of our own strength in our own strength only places us more on the path of death than we were before, although now we might do it under a religious umbrella with spiritual language.

God isn't against us. He's not calling us to die to ourselves because he's angry with us. The opposite is true. He's trying to get us to unwrap the dead ways of being that have surrounded us, bound us, and blinded us our whole life. This is not something we can do ourselves. We need help.

Jesus commanded Lazarus to come forth, but he didn't command him to take his own grave clothes off. He couldn't. That took others.

If all we've known is trusting in our own strength, then we have no experience discerning what to kill and what to let live within our hearts and in our lives. Apart from God, we will kill things that are not a problem to God, or we'll tolerate things in our lives that will kill us. We need spiritual discernment. Paul writes how his own conscience didn't condemn him, but he couldn't trust it. He needed the Spirit.

Paul instructs us to put to death our own works by the Spirit (Romans 8:13). The Holy Spirit must guide on the process. Relying upon the Spirit also includes the Spirit within others, their gifts from the Spirit.

God's goal isn't to obliterate us but to remove all aspects of our character that are keeping us from living the new creation waiting to burst forth in purpose and miracle. The latter is what he wants because he loves us and others around us.

In our own strength, we'll either say every desire and thought is evil (legalism) or that God wants me to be happy and therefore every desire is valid and justified (licentiousness). Both extremes are a lie. My desires and thoughts aren't always evil. Neither are they always good. They simply are, and if I reject them all or accept them all, those are both the same path to destruction.

God is out to redeem our desires and renew our thinking. So how do we know what to follow, what is valid, and what is true? The Spirit is the one leading us into all truth. He's the one to tell us what must be cut out and unwrapped and what we should leave and let be.

But surgery hurts. Discipline hurts. Even Jesus didn't enjoy it. We'd be perverted if we liked it. This isn't about masochism.

We endure the discipline, suffering and dying to self for one reason. We see the life and joy from it.

Life and Death

Now that we've been born again, entered the Kingdom of God, and are filled with the Spirit, we have the revelation of life. We have the eternal perspective showing us what is of life and what is of death through our relationship with he who is the Way, the Truth, and the Life. That relationship allows us to take every desire, thought, preference, and more and hold it up to the light of the Spirit to compare.

Thoughts, desires, and actions which aren't consistent with the wisdom and life of the Spirit, we now know to reject, or as the Bible puts it, consider them dead.

The ways of the world, its thinking and systems, including our strength and nature, all of it is already dead. They might be flopping around like a zombie, but they're dead. With the truth of that, we consider ourselves dead to those things. We don't make ourselves dead, neither do we decide what is dead, it just is. When we consider them dead, we are simply agreeing with the Spirit who gives us all truth.

The Bible tells us when we repented, we died, our nature and desire to sin was crucified with Christ (Galatians 2:20). Yet we still feel those temptations and the pull of those selfish wants.

When a person loses a limb, like a leg, they will still feel pain in the part that's missing. The foot hurts, even though the foot is gone. The knee aches or itches, but it's not there. It's called a phantom limb. The feeling is all in the brain. The mind has lived with that limb for years, the whole life until that point, and the mind takes time to adjust.

Our sin nature is the same. It's been crucified with Jesus. It's gone, as is its power over us. However, our minds have lived with the control of that sin nature our whole lives. What must change is our way of thinking. We must remind ourselves of what is already dead and rest in the finished work of Christ.

Carry the Cross

While in this life, we will deal with temptations and desires contrary to the will of God. Temptations and desires do not make us sinners. Jesus was tempted beyond any of us and expressed a will contrary to the Father's in Gethsemane (Matthew 26:39), and he lived without sin. Temptation and a will opposite of the Spirit isn't sin. When we allow those ways of death to have their way and we participate, that's unrighteousness.

Dying to self is a continual way of life. It's not something we pray once and then never deal with again. God is always working, shaping, and leading us through the process of living a new life in him.

> **Dying to self is a continual way of life. It's not something we pray once and then never deal with again.**

Having to die to self doesn't mean we're not living in new life, either. They work together. Die to my way and follow Christ, who is The Way.

To what do we die? Paul gives us a list in his letters, and they shouldn't surprise us. Pride, lying, sexual misconduct, division, anger, rage, greed, and idolatry (Colossians 3:5-9).

We die to having our own way, which includes personal and cultural preferences even if those ways are not evil. The food I enjoy eating, the music I enjoy or my Irish heritage can all be beautiful. However, if I try to have power over others and force them to abide by my preferences or culture, then that isn't of God. To mix worldly culture, politics, and preferences with the Gospel is to speak a lie, and lies aren't of God.

Another aspect of dying to self is in our reliance upon intellectualism or emotionalism. Most people, based on personality and individual strengths, attempt to engage in Christianity through either emotion or intellect. The cross offends both. God's not against our emotions or intellect, he created them, but it is a form of idolatry for them to attain primacy in our lives. Both our intellect and emotions find their security and purpose in submission to Christ, the one who created them, and they are alive when redeemed anew by the Spirit. Now they serve God instead of the other way around.

Paul was able to live free, not bound even to his own preferences, culture, or personality (1 Corinthians 9:22). He purposefully moved between cultures, appreciating and abiding by different ways of speaking and dress to make sure none of it hindered declaring the eternal Gospel. If Paul had been bound to his own culture and preferences, he couldn't effectually express the Good News.

The Kingdom of God has its own culture, a much better one, and it isn't about coercion or force. If anyone could force us to do what he said, it's God, and he doesn't. Neither should we.

Dying to self isn't an end. It's the beginning, a necessary part of living in the resurrection. The road is difficult, even a fight at times, but infinitely worth it.

Exploration

Serving others is a hallmark of the faith and a way we live when dying to ourselves.

Again, self-sacrifice isn't the goal, but a step. Others will be healed and blessed. Our lives will be filled with great joy in purpose and being a part of the bigger Kingdom story.

Jesus knelt, stripped naked, and washed feet as an example of how to live (John 13:1-17). Humble. Dying to self isn't feeling bad about ourselves. Not at all. God abundantly loves and values us. It is his pleasure to adopt us in the family.

We do this because our life is already seated at the right hand of God in Christ (Colossians 3:3). We already have that secure position. Why do we need a worldly one? We don't. Don't sit at the best seat at the table. Sit at the least important seat.

To be sure, we can serve with a selfish attitude, possibly for fame or notoriety, but Jesus teaches to serve in secret as much as possible (Matthew 6:1-4). Doing acts of service from a selfish motivation negates the good, according to the perspective of heaven. It becomes as if we never did it. God will glorify and reward what is good from the right motivation.

Where do you serve? Do you serve only at events or also as a lifestyle? I guarantee there are opportunities in every relationship you have, as well as events and organizations around you. Take advantage of every opportunity.

Father, thank you for revealing the dead that surrounds, binds, and blinds us. Teach us what to remove and give us the strength to test every thought and decision by your Spirit. Amen.

Chapter 21
Reveal the New

There are two kinds of stories. Every story is about transformation or the absence of it. In classic literature, a comedy is where characters believe a lie, causing disruption and conflict. The resolution is when the characters of the story reject the lie and discover the truth though the call to adventure. Whether action, science fiction, or romance, the genre may change but the core remains. The story ends when the transformation is complete. Pinocchio becomes a real boy. Rudy plays in a game for Notre Dame.

A tragedy is when the main character believes a lie, is confronted with the truth but rejects it, clinging to the lie. He or she receives the consequence of believing a lie.

Either way, the truth wins. Truth can't be adjusted or redefined, otherwise it is no longer truth. A perspective or an opinion might have value, but it's not the truth. The truth of God is immovable and not subject to the ways or changes in this world. Thank God. We couldn't count on it or feel secure in it otherwise.

Narratives in books, movies and even video games follow this rule of story and make billions of dollars every year. These ideas attract us because they ring true. It is a tragedy to live a life without meaning or change. Transformation makes the obstacles and pain worth it, gives our life meaning in a way that lasts beyond us, connects us to a bigger story and provides us and others hope.

Our life in Christ is a series of transformations, and yet it is also based on a finished work. In Christ, we are already at the right hand of God, and at the same time, we grow from faith to faith and strength to strength (Romans 1:17). We are being and becoming at the same time. More succinctly, we are becoming more the person we were born again to be, and already are in Christ. We are becoming the person God thought about before the foundation of the world—the person God works within and through for the world and eternity to see.

We can't redeem or transform the grave clothes. They must be removed.

The Father parents us according to the person he designed us to be. What gets in the way are the bindings and the blindness of the thinking and ways of this world and our own brains.

We can't redeem or transform the grave clothes. They must be removed.

Hear, Do, Walk

We can't only remove what is dead. That is only half the process, incomplete. We must step into this new life and replace the dead with what is alive.

Ephesians describes it as *putting on* the new person (Ephesians 4:24). As mystical as it may sound, it is an active process. We must choose to participate in the power and grace given to us. What is that process?

Jesus is a priest, the Great High Priest as described in Hebrews, the mediator between God and us. With his Spirit within us, we are a kingdom of priests, a concept we know as the *priesthood of all believers* (1 Peter 2:4-5). Our role with the world and others is to stand in the gap, to pray and intercede on behalf of those we love for their salvation and growth in Christ.

In the Old Testament, priests were anointed with two things. First, the blood of a sacrifice. A part of the ordination was to take blood and anoint the lobe of the ear, the thumb of the hand, and the big toe. But there was a second anointing, one of oil, on the same three places–ear, thumb, and toe (Leviticus 14). As priests through Christ, this anointing now applies to us.

We all know the blood of the sacrifice is symbolic of the forgiveness of God through Jesus, and the oil is the power of the Holy Spirit.

The ear, thumb, and foot. Why those three? Because we first hear the voice of God, then we obey his instruction, and constant obedience is following God. Hear, do, and walk.

This is the process of *putting on* the new person in Christ. We take what we find in Christ and clothe ourselves with tenderhearted mercy, loving-kindness, humility, gentleness, and patience (Colossians 3). We give generously and speak what is good and helpful when we talk (Ephesians 4). This is the fruit of the Spirit, the natural result and outgrowth of a life rooted in Christ.

To unwrap the walking miracles within us and others, we must refuse to preach or make appeals to the human nature through intellectualism or emotionalism. We can draw large crowds by those appeals, but we won't make or grow new people with them. Truth is found by the revelation of God through the Spirit. Paul makes it clear he refused to base his preaching of the Gospel on human reasoning (1 Corinthians 2:1-5). Human reasoning is not evil, but reason and emotion are insufficient foundations for the Gospel. Instead, Paul revealed the Spirit through his speaking and actions to build the right foundation on the eternal Christ and not human ability.

Lazarus heard Jesus and started walking out of the grave, and he quickly understood what needed to be removed (the grave clothes) to walk free. Once we start walking and doing what we hear from heaven, we find out what's getting in our way of walking in the freedom to which Christ calls us. Walking in his freedom helps us know what to remove.

As a new person in Christ, we must make allowances for the faults of others. God has forgiven us of great weakness and corruption, and we must do the same to be like him. When we know our propensity to sin and evil, we can easily relate to others with the same or similar struggles, for we have all fallen short of the standard (1 Peter 4:8).

The church in Corinth was messed up. They were divided, selfish, and practically celebrated sexual sin as a mark of love and grace. Sound familiar?

In 1 Corinthians, Paul addressed those moral failings, but his argument was continually a call to their identity in Christ. "You can deal with these squabbles between you. Don't you know you will judge angels?" "No one is of Apollos or Paul. You are all of Christ!" "Don't you know your body is the house of God?"

People will fail, as will we, but the correction should be to remind us of our own identity first. That gives the proper context and mindset for how we should live heaven on earth.

Finding the Gift

Now that we are in the process of hearing, doing, and walking, we discover our individual gifts and purposes. As we walk with Christ, patterns emerge. We exhibit different strengths and supernatural expressions. In essence, with the Spirit given to us, we have access to every gift, but God gives a special distribution of those gifts in ways that make us diverse and unique.

We each have the Spirit, but we can't say we don't need each other. The hand can't say to the foot, "I don't need you." We are parts of the body meant to unify and express Jesus as a whole (1 Corinthians 12). The gifts are part of that design and are given to edify the church, both the local assembly and beyond. This means we can't know our spiritual gift apart from the community of faith. No part of our physical bodies exists to give life to itself. Each member supports or brings nutrients to another. The gifts are the way the body of Christ edifies itself.

Sometimes we know what our gift is. Perhaps God reveals it to us individually. Most of the time, we need the body of Christ to help us recognize our gift. This isn't a personality or talents test we take. It is something we are told out of relationship with people who see us live our lives more than an hour a week sitting in a chair.

With our kids, my wife and I continually try to help our kids discover what their talents are, not assuming because they have our DNA that they are limited to what came before. They are each unique individuals with great potential. Sometimes they are surprised when we say, "Hey, you're really good at that." Then we challenge them to work on that talent through some type of training, investing in that talent.

In the family of God, we ask others, "What am I doing when you see Jesus in me?" The answer often surprises us. Because our focus is not on ourselves but on Jesus, following him, and serving others, we may not know when we are operating in a spiritual gift. Some are obvious like tongues or prophecy, and others are more difficult to determine. The community of God, who loves us, will help us discover our gifts, one or many.

The Kingdom community can give better opportunities and mentorship in the spiritual gift, challenge us to grow and hold us accountable. The church needs each gift, and the fuller expression of those gifts brings the whole body into more power and love.

Our gifts are not only to bless others, but to teach the body how we can all operate in our gifts. Paul gives a list of leadership gifts in Ephesians–pastors, teachers, apostles, prophets, evangelists. He then gives the purpose for those gifts. These gifts aren't to give people titles and professional positions or to excuse others from operating in these gifts. The leadership gifts are to teach the whole church how to do the work of the ministry (Ephesians 4:11-12). The very goal of an evangelist is to teach everyone how to better evangelize. An apostle shows how to lay a spiritual foundation in others, and a prophet to speak the words of God. Teachers teach how to explain the mysteries of the kingdom, and pastors display how to lead in service and self-sacrifice.

> **Our talents and personalities can't become excuses to not participate in what God wants us to do.**

Every person reborn from heaven has been given a gift for all. This isn't based on our natural ability or education or intellect. It's based on the power of God.

One of my favorite podcast conversations was with a friend, Joan, who encourages and ministers among people with disabilities. Too often those with disabilities are marginalized in the church, as if they can't serve or don't have anything to give because of their physical, intellectual, or emotional disability. But we forget that God isn't impressed with my ability to see, walk, hear, or what have you. We all serve from the power of the Spirit, and he gives gifts to all. We should include the gifts of all people, regardless of their age or ability, because their inclusion will bless the whole church.

Redeemed Talents

We must be careful with our natural talents and personality. God wants to use them, but since they are of our worldly nature, they must be redeemed and given to God in such a way that they aren't limiting factors our a source of pride in our own abilities. For example, I am mostly an extrovert. Can God use my extroverted personality? Of course. He often does. But I'm not limited by my extroverted personality or any talent I have when God leads me in other ways.

Talents and personalities are awesome, and given by God, but they can also become comfort zones in which we struggle to break free. Our talents and personalities can't become excuses to not participate in what God wants us to do. Just as spiritual gifts are supernatural and beyond our ability, our individual purpose within God's great singular purpose will also be a narrative of God's glory and power, not anything for which we can take credit.

God's plan for us will be vastly different from what we imagined as a kid. For me, even though God's call was clear, I fought being a teacher in a public school. I had a different plan but found joy in following God's path for me. Later, I resisted coming back to America from Korea and definitely fought becoming a church planting pastor, wrestling with God, as it were. I set out a few fleeces for that one, for sure. Each time, God corrected my thinking, and when I followed his path and purpose, there was joy and mystery and adventure.

The Father doesn't call us to do things we can do on our own. What would be the point? His plans for us are bigger than we are capable of accomplishing, which makes us uncomfortable and constantly reliant upon his voice and power to take each next step. Our story becomes based in what God has done, not us.

That's the transformation, to live on purpose with God, allowing him to change our story. The tragedy would be to reject a life of wonder and adventure for things that don't last.

The world doesn't need more religious leaders with religious titles. I'm saying that as one of them. The world needs people alive in the dreams and purposes of God. It needs reborn people walking with the Father in stories of miracle and joy among a world of tragedy and grief. In fact, many professional ministers miss out on the wonder of God speaking through practical work and careers. God constantly taught me truth while I was a public school teacher, in marketing, or a dozen other jobs throughout my life.

That's why the question is no longer, "What was I born to do?" Instead, now we ask, "What was I reborn to do?" There's a huge difference.

Exploration

God loves us so much he prepared redemptive works for us way before we started following him. How do you discover them?

First, listen to the voice of God. Hearing his voice is at the core of a life with God.

Second, we serve. We may not know exactly what God has for us, but I guarantee there are opportunities to start serving right where you are. God can't steer a parked car, so get moving in some capacity. Be generous with your time and abilities, giving with nothing in return.

What you will find is that opportunities pop up out of nowhere, or so it seems. God will correct your path and lead you to the purpose he has for you, but it won't happen if you're sitting on your behind and not actively listening. God's new pathways will stretch and challenge you. Guaranteed.

Third, check with believers you trust and who know you well. Ask them what they think about these new opportunities. God's voice is the one that counts most, but he often speaks through the family of Jesus followers around us.

Father, thank you for how you help us put on that new creation, our own expression of Christ. Continue to lead and teach us how to live in relational obedience with you and fulfill the plans and purposes you have for us. Amen.

Chapter 22
The Purpose of the Disciplines

There's always the training montage. Watch any sports movie, especially from the 80s, and you'll see the series of clips showing how the athlete finally gets motivated and serious about training hard. Usually there's a cheesy rock song to go along with it, something with lyrics like, "Keep on going! Don't give up!"

The most famous of these is *The Karate Kid*, where Miyagi is teaching Daniel karate by washing and waxing cars. Daniel must also paint the house and fence, and sand the deck. The realization on young Daniel-san's face when, because of his training, he can finally block Miyagi's punches and kicks is classic.

Back when I played basketball in high school, I hated the drills and exercises. I hated running around in circles for no apparent reason. I loved to play the games and scrimmage but thought some of the drills were dumb. In one exercise, we sat with our backs against the wall—staying there for what was probably seconds but felt like hours. My legs burned. I really didn't like that one.

But when I could dunk the basketball a little easier a few months later, I realized why we did that exercise.

We know we're supposed to do things like go to church, read the Bible, pray, and more. But we often feel like failures doing them.

Here's the secret. No one is good at discipline, not initially. In fact, we're going to be bad at it at first. That's part of the process.

On vacation, I took some time to go shoot around at an outdoor basketball court, and my 4-year-old son wanted to go with me. I took him, and of course, he wanted to take some shots, too. He missed everything, barely getting to the rim on most of his efforts.

I turned around to see him dejected and sitting against the fence off the court. "What's the matter, buddy?"

He said, "I'm losing."

God gave me the words in the moment, and I repeated them. "No, you're not losing, you're learning."

God will deliver us immediately from some issues. For others, he allows us to wrestle and learn over time to strengthen our character. We get stronger in faith through the fight, through resistance. Both are his work and by his Spirit.

> **Here's the secret. No one is good at discipline, not initially ...**

The disciplines within Christianity are difficult, and when we feel like we fail, we think these practices are for pastors or the really spiritual, not for us. But they are for every follower of Christ. We shouldn't need a job in the ministry to have the motivation to participate in these disciplines. That's a gross misunderstanding of their purpose and importance.

Disciplines of Faith

Why aren't we consistent with these disciplines? One main reason, we don't understand the why.

Why is an important and complex question. We all know when our kids learn to ask "why?" They repeat the question ad nauseam, which leads to the answer we hated as kids, but repeat out of sheer frustration, "Because I said so."

"Because I said so" isn't good enough, relating to the disciplines, or it only gets us so far, not like Christ. We have a Father who's training us to rule and reign with him in heaven, and the *why* part of the equation is essential. Answering the why gives us wisdom, understanding, and a greater perspective.

There was a video on social media that was a great example of changing perspective. Perhaps you saw it. A woman has been color blind her whole life. Someone gives her a pair of glasses that allow her to see in color for the first time in her life. Placing them on her head, she peers through them.

She weeps. She breaks down. She sees green. Blue. It's like she's seeing the world again for the first time, the same but new, and I can't help but shed a tear with her.

The disciplines aren't the goal; they are the means to an end. The spiritual practices are ways to focus and strengthen our faith.

Faith is the perception and the pursuit of the unseen. The unseen is the heavenly realm, the kingdom of God. It is the spiritual reality that surrounds us beyond any natural ability to see, hear, or engage with it. Faith is a gift from God. We couldn't see, hear, or pursue him without his grace and power. Faith is both perception and pursuit, working together. We can't pursue the eternal without being able to see it, and if we see it without pursuing it, then it's all for nothing.

Spiritual disciplines declare the unseen is more real than what we see. At the same time, they are the way to perceive this whole other world through faith so we can better walk closely with the Father. Did you notice how those work together? When we act as if the unseen is real, we see it better. That's what the disciplines teach us.

We all know the disciplines. Prayer, meditation, reading the Bible, fasting, serving others, gathering with other believers in fellowship and teaching, singing songs of worship, and giving. Others have added practices like confession, celebration, and study. We're going to use a couple as examples to show how they declare the power of the unseen.

Gathering with the believers affirms them as our family, even if we aren't connected by blood, culture, nationality, or anything of this world. When we meet for worship, teaching, prayer, and fellowship, we are acting like we have the same Daddy.

Giving says we have access to the wealth of heaven because of our Father and we understand God is our source of provision, not ourselves or our work. We give from heaven's wealth and lose nothing.

We only gain through generosity. Giving also helps make our loyalty and priority to the Kingdom, not the world, clear.

When we sing songs of worship, we are addressing a person we can't see with our eyes but know through faith, and we participate in an activity that constantly occurs in heaven around the throne.

The Scripture is God-breathed, inspired, and infused with the Holy Spirit over thousands of years, dozens of writers, and two main covenants. Yet the message is cohesive and redemptive. Reading the Bible declares we believe God reveals himself to us, and he hasn't changed over time. The Scripture is an avenue to better hear the voice of the Spirit of God.

Jesus said to the Jewish religious leaders in John 5, "You search the scriptures because you think there's life in them. These are the scriptures that testify of me, but you wouldn't come to me so you could truly have life!"

Years ago, I made a commitment to read through the whole Bible in a year. Part of my discipline was to listen to the Scripture on audio. At a particular passage, God began to reveal to me deeper truths from a verse. It distracted from the listening, however, so I turned up the Bible to drown out the voice of God.

Thankfully, God quickly corrected me. "This is the whole point," he said. "To hear my voice." I repented, turned off the audio, and listened while God began sharing more of himself with me.

Strengthening and focusing the muscles of faith, that's why we follow the disciplines.

Endurance

I've always wanted to run a marathon. Spoiler alert: I still haven't. But years ago, I had a colleague who ran marathons, and I expressed the desire. She asked me, "How much do you run now?"

I said, "Oh, I run three to four times a week, from 5 to 7 miles each time."

She told me, "If you regularly run 7 miles, you can run a marathon."

This surprised me. She explained how running a marathon is partly physical, but mostly mental. If I've run 7 miles, then I've pushed past the point where my body got exhausted and my mind said, "Quit!" Pushing past that point is the secret. I may not win the marathon or do it competitively, but I could run one.

People regularly state their belief when it comes to disciplines of faith. "I can't pray very long without falling asleep … I can't read more than a couple of verses without my mind wandering … I can't give because I have other responsibilities … I can't get to a meeting with other believers because I'm too busy …" and so on. For anyone who has said or thought these things, welcome to the club. We all do.

Paul describes our Christian walk as an athlete prepares for a competition (1 Corinthians 9:24), as a farmer plants and tends crops (James 5:7) or as a soldier trains for battle (2 Timothy 2:4). These are consistent and challenging endeavors that take priority because of the goal. An Olympic athlete doesn't go to parties and eat or live like everyone else, not if they want to win. A farmer gets up early, before anyone else, to tend to his crop. A soldier doesn't live like a common citizen. They are always alert and ready for battle. It's a different kind of life that requires discipline and strict commitment.

Self-discipline and self-control are fruit of the Spirit. If you've noticed the pattern, we can't participate in the disciplines in our own power. Disciplines push us to the point where we come against our own limits, perceived or real. Going beyond those limits is a form of dying to self, admitting that our activities and abilities are insufficient for the task. Disciplines help us grow in active faith, and this further builds our character and spiritual fortitude.

Paul says that he beats his own body into submission, meaning he claims freedom and dominion over his own desires and perceived needs. If we give in to our desires, doing what we want, then we aren't free, at least not walking in the freedom given to us.

If we tell our desires, "no, you don't need to watch that show or go to that concert or pay for that newer item, etc.," now we're able to replace that with what is true and needed. We allow God to take the reins over our desires for good through the Spirit by saying, "What I need is the fellowship of the saints, to learn better how to hear the voice of God, to give to those in need and please my Father, to sing a song of praise, to calm my soul and spend time in prayer."

Our desires make demands in the now for the now. The Spirit leads us to make choices in the now that bring benefit for the now and the later, and the past as well. In the right mindset and motivation, the benefits of those disciplines are eternal. The eternal blessings are those that span all chronological time.

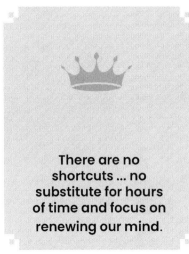

> There are no shortcuts ... no substitute for hours of time and focus on renewing our mind.

There are no shortcuts. We love shortcuts. How can I get a full-time salary on part-time hours? Pyramid schemes make this appeal all the time. But there's no substitute for hours of time and focus on renewing our mind.

Malcom Gladwell postulated in his book *Outliers* that a person masters something after doing it for 10,000 hours. He tested his theory in various narratives. What if we took that approach to renewing our mind according to the eternal perspective?

Most people don't do this, of course, hence the narrow way. It seems easier to admit our failures and live life in weakness. This mindset doesn't lead us to our purposes and callings, and it doesn't bring us the joy and peace we can't lose. Since the seemingly easier way is based on our own abilities, taking that path brings us more anxiety and inner conflict, undermining the gift of faith we've been given, not strengthening it. We see less of the unseen realm, and with the lack of faith and hope, we are more discouraged and defeated.

The God of the impossible specializes in second chances. It's not hopeless when we fail, fall, or quit because he's always inviting us back to a relationship with him based in his ability, not ours. The Spirit of God is eternal and will endure by his nature. Our endurance in our walk with God and spiritual disciplines is based on the Spirit. Call on him. Ask for his help. The Father gives good gifts, especially the Holy Spirit.

And the gift of the body of Christ.

With God and Others

There are some things God will not give us from the community of faith. We only get them from him directly. There are other things God will not give us alone. We only get them from the gathering of the believers and their spiritual gifts.

All discipline is rooted in individual self-discipline. To consistently be a part of a community, I need self-discipline.

We weren't meant to participate in these disciplines alone. Some of them we simply can't. Gathering with other Christians necessitates a group of people, and the best way is still getting together in person. Giving needs someone to receive our gift.

For other disciplines, there is great power and revelation if we take part in them together. God will share different insights with different people who join together and edify one another. The giving in Acts resulted in no one having lack. I can sing to God alone, but there is something amazing about a group of people lifting voices to the throne together. The biggest book in the Bible is Psalms, a book of worship. We can't love one another as Christ has loved us without other people around us.

On a practical level, others will give us tips and encouragements from their walk that empowers our own.

Participating in worship and other disciplines with our brothers and sisters in Christ is a more complete expression of heaven. God isn't divided. He's three in one, and no one worships God alone in heaven. Our expression of the disciplines in unity and love helps us to see and understand the unseen, heavenly Kingdom more, and it bolsters our peace and boldness.

The body of Christ, when operating as it should, also spurs us on to greater commitment and personal discipline, encouraging us in our gifts and helping us when we momentarily fail. This is what family does. In so doing, we prepare ourselves and each other for the mission ahead.

Exploration

I'm not big on everyone having the same structure concerning the disciplines, as in, "pray for ten minutes, read one chapter, and then journal for two pages." That might work in the beginning, for the very immature, but that shouldn't last long.

To have the same structure and amount of discipline for everyone, like a formula, is conformity. Conformity is the way of the world. The Spirit is about transformation.

To not participate in the disciplines at all is legalism, as well. We've been given them for a purpose, to grow in the perception and pursuit of the unseen realm.

You should pray, read the Bible, gather with followers of Christ, and give generously. How much? Ask God. He will tell you (2 Corinthians 9:6-7). And here's a guarantee—it'll be more than you think you can give. God doesn't teach us how to rest in the Spirit and walk by faith by asking us to do what we are able to do without him.

Let God stretch you and push you in the various disciplines. Seek his input and wisdom as your Rabbi and Father in how and what to participate in the training for eternity.

Father, thank you for training us as your kids to rule and reign with you. Give us the wisdom and insight in how to apply ourselves to spiritual disciplines, and help us endure, dying to self, and walk in life and peace. Amen.

Chapter 23
The Mission

God gave me a vision, a waking dream of sorts, before my wife and I went to Korea.

A friend prayed over me one night after a community worship time. While he prayed, God showed me a map of Korea. A blue line arced over the map toward Korea. The line hit the center of Korea and exploded out in a big bright ball. To me, an 80s kid, it looked like the computer simulation of the nuclear missile attack from the movie *War Games*. God told me that it wasn't a destructive image. He was sending us to Korea to spread light, truth, and love, all in his power. I shared this picture with my friend, my wife, and others, encouraged that God was with us and going out ahead of us.

We did see God move and change lives in miraculous ways. We experienced healing in ourselves and others, God filling people with his Spirit, salvations, deeper dedications of believers, and discipleship.

Of course, it was also incredibly difficult at times, and we wouldn't have endured without the hope of the purpose and the mission before us.

Not everyone is called by God to move overseas and teach at an international school. However, every individual reborn from heaven has been given a mission within the purpose of God. And God hasn't kept this a secret. He's made it clear.

The Purpose and the Mission for the Reborn

Let's begin with a distinction between purpose and mission. In a broad sense, purpose is the *why* and mission is the *how*. To repeat the purpose, the Father is reconciling all creation back to himself through his Son, the Lord Jesus Christ. To reconcile, Jesus also undoes the works of the Devil.

Now that we are reborn from the will of God, we have inherited his purpose. There is a Kingdom, and we are being trained and discipled by God to rule and reign with him in the New Heaven and Earth.

Why have we been reborn from the Father? To reconcile all back to the Father through the Lord Jesus Christ and to undo the works of the Devil. We were reborn for this.

The Bible gives us our mission, our part, within that purpose. Paul calls it the ministry of reconciliation. We are to entreat, beg, and communicate to the world how they should be reconciled to the Father (2 Corinthians 5:18).

The mission of the reconciled is to call others to the same reconciliation. We have been invited into the Redemptive Story of God to invite others to change their story, too. We have been rescued to participate in the rescue of others.

> **We have been invited into the Redemptive Story of God to invite others to change their story, too.**

There are countless ways to be involved in the Mission of God. For my wife and me, through that season of life, our part of the mission was to move overseas and teach. Before that time, we were already participating in the mission through other avenues. And when God moved us on from Korea and back to the US, we continued living on mission in other ways. The seasons and individual roles may change, but the mission remains.

Through our lives, our words, and our deeds, we communicate the message of Christ. Be reconciled to God.

We don't discipline ourselves through prayer, reading the Bible, fasting, giving our money, etc, for some sort of individual self-actualization. We require that discipline because we have a mission ahead of us, and we must be ready.

Personal

Before going to Korea, I read a disturbing passage in Exodus. God had called Moses from the burning bush, and despite some argument, Moses obeyed and took his family. Then God came to kill Moses on the way to Egypt (Exodus 4:24-26).

Um, what? Moses had obeyed and went to Egypt. Why was God going to kill him? I was also obeying the call to another country, and the passage in Exodus seriously disturbed me.

Back to the Scripture, Moses' wife awoke and circumcised their sons. Quite the wake-up call. Once the circumcision was done, God relented and didn't kill them.

I wrestled with God on this. In the days of Exodus, circumcision was a sign of the Abrahamic Covenant, that the nation of Israel was set apart to God. In the New Covenant, Paul says this is a circumcision of the heart (Romans 2:25-29). Our hearts must be set apart, holy, and dedicated to God. This is an inner reality.

Without this focus and primary work, we will be easily manipulated by outside forces, attempting to find our rest and security elsewhere. Even good things become an idol.

Build the Church

Upon reaching Korea, my wife and I got involved in the local church. We didn't church-hop and see what worked best for us. We asked God, and he gave us clarity on where we were to invest ours time and relationship. Initially, there weren't any opportunities to use what I would call our *spiritual gifts*. God clearly told us to start serving somewhere, anywhere, and love people. We did, and over time, the opportunities arose for us to encourage and disciple others with our spiritual gifts.

The Church, universal and local, is the outpost of heaven on earth, an eternal assembly of believers that will last beyond this world. We are built together upon the foundation of Christ, and we are wise to invest in what will last.

The mission of God includes relational discipleship, spiritual formation, or whatever a tradition might call it. We have been reborn into a family of God where we make more of ourselves. That requires relationship more than a program. The Jesus model of discipleship was life on life continual connection on mission together. Time and time again, God has revealed to me how discipleship happens when we intentionally live with our brothers and sisters in the family of God and teach one another about Christ from the Spirit.

This includes quality and quantity time together. In the Kingdom, we don't decide between quantity or quality. It's both/and.

One of the best ways to build the church is to add more kids.

Jerusalem, Judea, Samaria, and the World

God called my wife and me to a place where we looked different, acted different, and spoke a different language, all with the message to people, "God sent us to tell you that he loves you and wants you to be reconciled to him through Jesus Christ." We not only built the church through service and discipleship, but we engaged the community around us with the Gospel and saw God save people. We witnessed more people reborn while we joined God's story there in Korea.

The church isn't a country club or a clique. We are sent out to make the family bigger.

As an extension of the mission, it doesn't work if we keep it to ourselves individually or corporately. Christ left heaven to come to earth, the ultimate sending, and if we have his Spirit, then that's who we are. We are sent. Maybe not to Korea or another country, but outside of our comfort zones and to some people somewhere, perhaps as close as across the street.

The Abrahamic covenant was to bless all people of all nations, and the culmination of that reality is expressed in the first chapter of Acts where Jesus states that with his Spirit, those disciples would be witnesses unto God to Jerusalem, Judea, Samaria, and the ends of the earth (Acts 1:8). Those are increasingly bigger areas, from city to region to the next region to every place people exist.

This is a world-wide, world-changing mission. And even if we aren't individually called to go across the world, cross cultural communication and diversity is the mission of the whole church, and we can be part of it through prayer, giving, and encouragement. But we can't be separate from the world-wide aspect of the mission and be in Christ at the same time.

Spreading the Gospel cycles back to part 1 of this book, removing the stone so people can experience Christ for themselves. The Lord is faithful to do this work.

We were reborn to reconcile all of creation back to the Father.

We were reborn to reconcile all of creation back to the Father, first our own hearts, then the process of discipleship in community, and next going out unto the earth to engage people with that Gospel.

Exploration

It has never been easier to get involved in your community or around the world. With the advent of the internet, we almost have too much opportunity to be connected with all God is doing. But being overwhelmed isn't an excuse to do nothing.

Where can you begin? First, as usual, start with prayer and asking God for direction and revelation. He is faithful to reveal what spiritual wisdom. Jesus instructs us to pray for workers for the harvest. Participate in prayer.

Second, you've been called to a local church. Be faithful and consistent there and seek out where that group is involved in service or missions, whether in the local community or overseas or both. Join your local church family in those opportunities.

Third, take some direction from your gifts or skills. What are you good at? What are your natural skills? What are your spiritual gifts?

Do some research on opportunities related to the answers to those questions.

Remember, begin where you are and love who is around and in front of you, and God will give you joy on the mission with him. Then he will open other opportunities that stretch your faith and give you even more joy and peace on that mission.

Father, thank you for sharing your purpose with me and calling me on loving mission with you. Reveal to me your specific call and direction for my life to give generously of myself to others and see your wonderful work on the earth. Amen.

Chapter 24
The War

Die Hard, despite what some say, is a Christmas movie. John McClane is a New York cop that goes to a foreign land (California) to fight for his marriage and soon finds himself fighting bad guys to save his wife and others.

One of the most overlooked characters is Argyle, the limo driver. He's a nice guy, dropping John at the high-rise office building and waiting for him in the parking garage. While waiting, Argyle sits in the back of the limo and has a personal party, calling friends on the car phone, watching TV, and listening to music. He's so engaged in his own entertainment, in fact, he completely misses the massive battle going on right over his head. He's oblivious.

The news on the TV in the limo informs him of the battle taking place around him and he realizes how clueless he's been the whole time.

Many Christians are the same way. Stories have value, as we've already discussed, but the consumer-driven entertainment that permeates our culture often distracts us from what is important, namely the war that surrounds us.

The primary focus of God is people. God's purpose is the reconciliation of all things to the Father through the Son. We are eternal and created in his image. That's what God is after, to redeem it all. If we are to undo the works of the Devil in that process, do we really expect the enemy to make it easy on us?

There is resistance to our mission, an enemy, and we are involved in battles and war whether we know it or believe it or not. To follow Christ is to follow him into a spiritual war.

Jesus is a warrior (Revelation 19:11-16). God was called the Lord of Heaven's Armies in the Old Testament.

Conflict and crisis reveal who we really are, and we are like our Daddy and Savior–warriors. That's the Spirit within us, the Spirit that renewed and redeemed us. We were reborn to be in this fight, particularly empowered to seek and save.

Like Argyle, we act shocked when battle and crisis invade our lives, but we shouldn't be surprised. The Scripture declares an epic conflict, and we are needed. Each one of us. Lives hang in the eternal balance. We were reborn for this battle.

The War

The Devil isn't after our bank accounts, our careers, or cars. He may create crisis and attack us through those temporary things, but he knows what's important. He's after our souls and the souls of the people we love. He's after our neighbors and co-workers. The Devil would kill every one of us and throw us into eternal torment if he could, if there wasn't someone who is willing to fight him (Job 1).

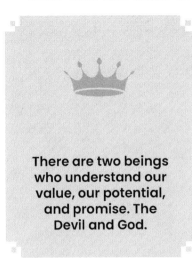

There are two beings who understand our value, our potential, and promise. The Devil and God.

There are two beings who understand our value, our potential, and promise. The Devil and God. Both will go to great lengths to accomplish their goals. The Devil seeks to steal, kill, and destroy, and God desires to give abundant, eternal life.

The enemy is terrified of beleivers activated as warriors of God's love and reconciliation, and he is dedicated to undermining or destroying our lives and purpose.

Because we will inherit a kingdom, we must understand other kingdoms exist, powers, authorities, both in this world and in the unseen realm (Ephesians 6:12). God will place all other authorities under the feet of Jesus, and Jesus will then hand everything back to the Father (1 Corinthians 15).

The battle between God and the Devil isn't much of a fight, to be honest. Satan started the whole war already beaten. He's not trying to win against God. He knows that's futile. The Devil is trying to hurt God by deceiving, stealing, destroying, and killing what God loves–people. Eternal souls of eternal value.

God isn't trying to beat the Devil, either. That's a done deal. His mission is that none should perish and go the way of Satan, death and corruption. He sent his Son so people who believe would have eternal life.

As his children who will inherit heaven, our training includes fighting this battle with him. Of the three levels of maturity in 1 John, one is for the young people to overcome the evil one. We must learn to care about and fight for what our Father does.

The world, the devil, our sin nature, and death, have all been beaten. People aren't our enemy, and we participate in a lie of the Devil when we act like they are. We battle the powers of the unseen realm, those that seek to destroy the souls of humanity.

In the Old Testament, God promised the land and the victory to Israel, and yet Joshua still had to cross the Jordan and lead the people of Israel into battle. A major theme of Jesus' ministry was to establish the right kingdom, the right authority over legions of demons oppressing people God loved (Matthew 12:22-29).

Make no mistake. We are in a fight. As we love people and lead them to the greatest gift of Jesus and the Father, we will face resistance, sometimes incredibly so. But to make an impact in the battle ahead, to overcome, we need to learn our weapons and how to use them.

The Weapons

The battle is with and in the unseen, spiritual realm. Therefore, we require weapons that have an effect in that realm. Too often we try to wage spiritual war with the things or systems of this world, but the weapons of this reality don't affect the heavenly one. We require spiritual power to make a difference. God has given us those weapons, and Scripture shows us how to fight this battle.

Obedience is a weapon. Hearing and obeying fights the chaos and crisis brought by demonic attack and influence. Paul calls these *weapons of righteousness* in our hands. (2 Corinthians 6:7)

Prayer undergirds every part of spiritual warfare. We do our most strenuous and effective battle in prevailing prayer. Yes, we pray for our needs, and we should. But we have been given prayer for so much more—as a weapon to cast down strongholds, to call on God to fight the battles with spirits, to give his gifts of faith and repentance to ourselves and others. Along with obedience, we can do great things in prayer. "The earnest prayer of a righteous person has great power and produces wonderful results." (James 5:16) Prayer gives us access to God's power. Let's use it for the eternal good of others.

Of course, we're all familiar with the armor of God (Ephesians 6:10-18), spiritual defenses and weapons to guard against and defeat the kingdom of darkness. Each piece of the armor is an aspect of the Spirit life. Nothing physical or material is mentioned.

The helmet of salvation provides us with the mind of Christ. The breastplate of righteousness represents how we protect our heart by following the Spirit. The belt reveals how we must bind ourselves to truth. Faith, perceiving and pursuing the unseen, is a shield that blocks the attacks of the Devil. The shoes of the Gospel empower us as people of the Father's purpose and mission. And the sword of the Spirit is the word of God, the Lord Jesus Christ, speaking the message of Christ from the Spirit.

If the armor of God is an example of the Jesus Model, how did he fight? He acknowledged the activity of the enemy, understanding there were evil, powerful, unseen forces at work to hurt and destroy people. Next, he directly addressed the demons with truth. The Devil's chief weapon is to lie, as he has from the beginning. The one offensive weapon, the Sword of the Spirit, is to listen and speak the words of God.

For example, the Devil lied to Jesus (Matthew 4:1-11), "Turn that stone into bread." Yes, it was a temptation, but every temptation is based on a lie. The lie (that his need for food should direct his actions) tempted him to disobey and use his power for his own gain (turn this stone into bread). There's nothing wrong with eating bread. Jesus did it so often, his critics called him a glutton. But the Spirit had led him into the wilderness to fast for 40 days. To eat, in that case, would have been disobedience.

But Jesus didn't address the temptation (turn the rock into food). He dealt with the lie behind it with truth, quoting from the Old Testament. "Man doesn't live by bread alone but every word that continually proceeds from the mouth of God." Bread satiates a temporary desire, but we will be hungry again. The words of God are eternal and give us deeper satisfaction than physical bread. On another occasion, after meeting the woman at the well, Jesus talks about bread again. When his disciples encouraged him to eat, they seemed offended that he wasn't hungry anymore. Jesus responds, "My food is to do the will of the one who sent me."

When we do battle with the Devil using the Word, it isn't random Scripture we throw at the enemy. That will get us into more trouble in spiritual warfare. We ask God for revelation about the lie behind what is going on, and then we speak to the spirit directly with the truth God reveals through us. We speak his words. Then we are fighting *with* God, battling with the one who has already won. It is way of victory.

Truth always comes with love. We are fighting for the souls of people, to heal and deliver others from the oppression, both spiritual and physical. Love is our greastest weapon and central to it all. Jesus didn't conquer or establish his rule and reign through force and coercion. That's oppression. We don't solve injustice with more injustice or oppression with more oppression. Jesus did it with love. He healed. He set free. He cast out demons. He fed the hungry and clothed the naked. He loved people.

Love never fails. Either that's hyperbole or it's true. I believe it's true, especially since they killed the God who is love and he just popped up out of the grave again three days later. No one can kill or stop God's love. There's no law that can contain it. Let's use the weapon of God's love without restraint or checking to see if any are worthy. We weren't worthy of it, either.

The Foxhole Effect

We fight with God, and at times, we do it alone. But we aren't meant to fight alone. We fight with other disciples.

David beat Goliath, but the army of Israel routed the Philistines immediately after. While in exile, David started gathering some questionable characters that became the mightiest warriors in history.

Jesus cast out demons regularly, but as he sent his disciples out to preach the Gospel of the Kingdom, they encountered spiritual resistance and also delivered people from evil spirits (Matthew 10:1). Jesus sent the disciples out in pairs, not alone (Luke 10:1).

During an attack, the enemy employs the lie, "You are all by yourself," as it happened to Elijah in the Bible (1 Kings 18:22). It happens to all of us. When we act on that lie, we isolate ourselves from others. Yet there is power in fighting together. One beats a thousand, so there is value alone, too, but two beat ten thousand. No wonder Jesus sent them out by two. The more we have alongside us in battle, the effect is spiritually exponential with each one added. By that spiritual math, are three 100,000?

Along with the power and safety of unity, we also enjoy more intimacy with God and others when fighting together.

Strength in numbers begins with going on mission together. First, we should take our families, our spouses and kids. Second, we should go with the church.

"We're talking about war, here," someone might say, "and you want to take kids into it?"

The Devil is already after our kids and family. They are already a part of the war. The safest place for anyone to be in that war is with the Father, and he is on mission. Go with him and with one another.

Along with the power and safety of unity, we also enjoy more intimacy with God and others when fighting together.

I call it the foxhole effect. Men who have shared a foxhole through intense battle share everything. They confess they end up fighting not for the greater cause, as much as to protect the man next to them. After the war, they explain how they feel closer to the man they shared battle with than their own families.

Our intimacy with God grows when we are on mission with him. That's where he is and what he's doing. It's sharing what's important to him, eternal souls and their redemption. It also brings families and communities of faith closer together in ways that fellowship and potluck dinners—as great and delicious as they are—just can't.

This isn't about choosing to be in the war. We're already a target with enemies all around. This is waking up to the reality and choosing to act out of love for souls that matter instead of hiding away in our distractions like Argyle in *Die Hard*.

Exploration

Finally, fighting in community provides people to help us when we fail and want to quit. Living the life of Christ is full of joy and wonder and miracle, but it can also be very difficult. Jesus promised we would have trouble, and trouble makes us tired. Exhausted. Ready to quit.

The Bible talks about endurance and not giving up several times. Tempting us to quit is one of the main strategies of the enemy. It's the best way to defeat us.

I guarantee you'll want to quit. Often. You might have experienced that this week or even today.

Jesus makes us another promise. He has overcome the world. He has not only overcome the problems of the world, but the very world containing the problems. He's already overcome it all.

That is difficult to remember when we are ready to give up.

When that happens, we need a community, people with us in the foxhole. We need people who validate how difficult it is, and say, "Yeah, I want to quit sometimes, too." We need a community that will not leave it there but will encourage us with the wonderful things God has done and has promised. They take us by the hand and give us hope, reminding us we aren't alone.

Father, thank you for providing the weapons and defenses we need to fight the enemy wanting to kill us. Give us wisdom and revelation to deal with the lies and attacks of that enemy and help us fight with love and truth and the Spirit. Amen.

Now I *Knower* It

*P*eter, don't you know who you are?

Wendy asked that question of the old man who needed to realize the hero he was.

Now I'm asking you.

Do you know who you are? Who you were reborn to be?

The hero. The cherished child of the King. The warrior of love.

In the narrative of Lazarus raising from the dead, we see the model of Jesus, how we were born again to be like the Son of God and …

CROW – to preach the love of the Father and the Kingdom of God by removing all worldly barriers as a community and to introduce the world to Christ.

FLY – our very nature changed to live free according to a new law, born again from that home beyond the skies.

FIGHT – to remove what is dead out of love and reveal the eternal through the transformation of our everyday life to intimacy and purpose, joining Christ in undoing the works of the Devil.

A friend of mine used a term in a morning devotional years ago. God was teaching her a truth that she knew, but through more revelation, she said, "Now I know*er* it."

Yes, it's a made-up word. But I've used it ever since. Biblically, *to know* is an intimate experience, far more than an intellectual exercise, a becoming one with someone.

My prayer is that if you've gone this far, then you *knower* your identity in Christ, the anointing you have within you, the divine DNA from the Father.

The secret is, even though God called me to write this book, I also must meditate and learn more. My mind must continue to be renewed according to what is eternally true. I must *knower* it, too.

I pray we *knower* it together as brothers and sisters.

Peace.

Acknowledgments

To God who is the source of all that is good. This book is from you and to you.

To Becca, my wife, my best friend, my partner, and love. There's no one I'd rather go on an adventure with than you.

To my children, Micah, Elisha, and Hosanna. You are each a unique joy and blessing to our lives and this world. My prayer is that you would each fall madly in love with Jesus more and more.

To my church in Suwanee. I love having an amazing family of God I can brag on wherever I go.

To my brothers and sisters at Phoenix Roasters. You are each a person I have learned from and benefited from in wisdom and community.

To the writing networks of which I'm a part: Serious Writer, Word Weavers, Realm Makers, Christian Authors Network. It is an undeserved and unlikely blessing for this misfit to find his people.

To the men and women who have invested what is of Christ into me. Larry Trammell, Alice Arraez, Chris Strong, John Taggart, Rose Palmer, and more. You have each given generously of your life and light and I would not be who I am without the gift of God in you.

Meet Britt Mooney

Great stories change the world. Britt Mooney loves to live and tell great stories. He and his wife served as missionaries in South Korea and has traveled to other countries for ministry.

Mooney is a pastor, author, and podcaster. He has phenomenal conversations about the Good News of the Kingdom with pastors, authors, missionaries, filmmakers, and more on his podcast, *Kingdom Over Coffee*. Check out his books and ministry on his website www.brittmooney.com. Mooney currently lives on God's adventure with his amazing wife, three creative kids, and their dog in Suwanee, GA.

Made in United States
Orlando, FL
18 August 2023